Walking to Cootehill

WALKING TO COOTEHILL

New and Selected Poems, 1958-1992

JOHN ENGELS

Middlebury College Press

Published by University Press of New England

Hanover and London

MIDDLEBURY COLLEGE PRESS

Published by University Press of New England, Hanover, NH 03755

© 1993 by John Engels

All rights reserved

Printed in the United States of America 5 4 3 2 1

CIP data appear at the end of the book

In Memory of

VINCENT ENGELS and

GEORGE LAHAGE

Newborn

The world displayed itself simply enough.
There were portents, of course,
the mirrors smoky and slow.
But I had no choice,

I was unpreventable.
A minute old, I was one history
of ten billion conflagrations,
my heart a chimney.

I was nothing
if not interested.

—for Henry Matthew Amistadi

Contents

Acknowledgments xiii

THE NAMING

Adam Signing 3
Adam Awakening 4
Watching for Animals 5
The Marshes at Suamico Wisconsin 6
Night Bird 7
The Naming 8
Cardinals 9
Muskrat 10
The Geese 11
The Crows 12
Snowy Owl 13
Damselfly, Trout, Heron 14
Apple Trees 15
Cobra 16
Love Poem 17
The Walled Garden 18
Details of the Frozen Man 19
The Guardian of the Lakes at Notre Dame 20
Locked Out 21
Falling on Blood Mountain 23
Sister Vincent 24
Clearing 25
At Night on the Lake in the Eye of the Hunter 26
The Raft 27
The Photograph 29
Turtle Hunter 32
When in Wisconsin 33
Feeding the Swans 34
Terribilis est locus iste 35
Olduvai 37
In Cedar Grove Cemetery 38
Beans 39
Bog Plants 40
Bullhead 41
The Fish Dream 42
Hagfish 43
Pigeons 44
Cardinals in the Ice Age 45
Traveling 46

Prince Mahasattva on Blood Mountain   48
With Zimmer at the Zoo   49
Silent Film   50
The Waiters at The Park Hotel, Belgrade   52
The Hunters   53
Taxi   55
Shark   56
Dead Pig   57
Walking to Cootehill   59
Picnic   61
Winter Flight   63
The Planet   65
At Dawn on Gun Point   66
Proofs of the Witholding   67
The Storm   68

THE UNNAMING

Aurora   71
Comet   72
Earth Tremor, the Sky at Night   75
The Weather   76
Damp Rot   77
Bad Weather on Blood Mountain   79
At the Top of Blood Mountain   81
Van Gogh Prophesies the Weathers of His Death   83
Earthquake   85
Foote Brook   86
Landslide   87
Waking from Nightmare   89
Black Dog   90
Devil's Hole   91
The Fire   93
The Morning News   95
The Recognition   96
The Revolutionary Museum in Ljubljana   97
Barking Dog   99
Saying the Names   101
Great Grandmother   102
Wakeful at Midnight   103
Ghosts   104
For Philip Stephen Engels   105

Distances   106
After Thirteen Years   107
Anniversary   111
The Silence, for John   113
Artesian   114
Long Ago   116
A Little Night Music for My Mother   117
The Warning   118
I Dream of Roy Hanna   119
Joyce Vogler in 1948   120
The Palais Royale Ballroom in 1948   121
Lonnie Peterson   123
The Ghosts at Red Banks   124
A Watercolor   125
The Fragonard, the Piéta, the Starry Sky   126
Mahler Waiting   130
A Reading   133
Spring Prophecy   134
Garden   136
In March   137
Meadow   138
East Middlebury   139
The Garden in Late Summer   140
Mountain Road   141
Orchard   142
Pilgrimage   143
Vivaldi in Early Fall   145
After Alcuin   147 ✔
The Electric Fence Game   149
Walker Mountain   151
In a Side Aisle of Kennedy Bros. Antiques Mall   154
Emergency   155
Landlord   156
Epitaph   157
Naturist Beach   158

Acknowledgments

The poems in the collection are drawn in part from previously published volumes:

The Homer Mitchell Place (1968), *Signals From the Safety Coffin* (1975), and *Blood Mountain* (1977), all published by the University of Pittsburgh Press; *Vivaldi in Early Fall* (1981), *Weather-Fear: New and Selected Poems, 1958–1982* (1983), both published by the University of Georgia Press; *The Seasons in Vermont* (1982), published by Tamarack Editions, Syracuse, New York; *Cardinals in the Ice Age* (1987), published by Graywolf Press, St. Paul, Minnesota; and *The Bread Loaf Anthology of Contemporary American Poetry* (1986), published by the University Press of New England.

The poems in *Walking to Cootehill* have appeared as follows:

Antioch Review: "Walking to Cootehill." *Boulevard*: "Ghost." *Crazy Horse*: "I Dream of Roy Hanna." *Ironwood*: "Beans." *Georgia Review*: "In Cedar Grove Cemetery." *Kenyon Review*: "Birthday Poem" (here retitled "Epitaph"), "Dead Pig," "The Spirits," "Newborn," "Skull," "Black Dog," "Night Bird." *The Nation*: "A Reading." *NER/BLQ*: "A Little Night Music for My Mother," "Long Ago," "Silent Film," "Naturist Beach." *New England Review*: "Locked Out," "In A Side Aisle of Kennedy Bros. Antiques Mall," "Waking from Nightmare," "Watching for Animals." *New Virginia Review*: "Landslide," "Meadow," "Feeding the Swans," "The Morning News" (part of which was published in an earlier version and in another form in *Carleton Miscellany*). *Poetry Ireland*: "Mountain Road." *Southern Review*: "Hagfish," "Details of the Frozen Man," "East Middlebury," "Turtle Hunter." *The Quarterly*: "The Warning," "Devil's Hole." *Poems for a Small Planet: Contemporary American Nature Poetry*: "In March," "Garden."

"Walker Mountain" is reprinted with the permission of the Notre Dame Sesquicentennial, © 1992 by the University of Notre Dame.

The author would like to express his appreciation to The Frost Place, to Annaghmakerrig, and to the Rockefeller Study and Conference Center at Bellagio, for providing time and space in which to work on this manuscript. He is indebted to the attentive and difficult readers he encountered at Bellagio, and especially—and as usual—to David Huddle and Sydney Lea for their ready willingness to read and to advise.

July 1992   J.E.

Walking to Cootehill

THE NAMING

Adam Signing

Here in the cool, birdlit realms,
his breath drawn out into the sky
which much as himself has come
to wish to breathe, he stands

on the cliff's verge, far short
of where the impulse to go on
might have lessened; and he stares
down on the Garden's silences,

not seeing her, who—in that instant
risen from the light of the yellow
seedling grasses—looks up at him
and cannot catch his eye or call out,

somehow signal, finding herself to be
faint and tremulous of voice,
the soft flesh of her hands
still taking place; and sees him make

suddenly, without warning, into the milky air
the difficult signs for *flight*, for
danger, as well as the simpler one
for *love*, not even thinking to be seen

or answered, and therefore
gesturing so swift, so gorgeously complex
into the calyx of the sky
that looking into the rushed

dance of his hands—in that first
most urgent measure of
those silences, she
could not well follow him.

—from *Vivaldi in Early Fall*, 1981

Adam Awakening

When I awakened
and found you beside me
and reached out to touch
the warm ridge of your spine,

it was then that the end,
the ineloquent function
began to demonstrate itself—
already the world was finished,

however measurable
the silence, however
the need did not lessen.
For now

I touch you with my hands
that are hands. Later
the dust will not forget
what it has loved.

—from *Vivaldi in Early Fall*, 1981

Watching for Animals

Had he been quicker, less
unbelieving, more willing
to look up, he would have seen

bears rise on their hind legs
from the tall grass
along the lake shore, elk

go skittish and alert,
swans flare from the rotting ice—loons,
whales, martens, everything

abruptly alarmed and winging,
sounding, clawing back
to the thronged hideouts, the bull

abruptly unkneeling to buck
white-eyed around the fences, cows
in the milk barns commencing

to bawl, sheep scared
into antic, trick and caper.
Instead, at dawn

his narrow window, by night
a mirror, began to clear,
and gradually revealed

the shorn world, empty
of the animals which had bounded
into being and out again

in the one teeming instant
between his glance to and away
from an odd agitation of some

meadow grasses, which, scarcely
grazed by his eye, and without
mediation, resolved to a nibbling hare.

The Marshes at Suamico Wisconsin

At the edge of the marshes the cattails leaped with frogs.
One of us found twined on a sedge a tiny green snake,
a vigor of grassy light burning its slow way out,
picked it up, let it coil on her palm,
wave its head, flicker its coral tongue—

carried it so for awhile until it grew frightened,
tensed and gave off for so small a thing
a remarkable high-flavored reek. She flung it away,
and none of us ever could find it again,
though we kept on the lookout. Then, deeper,

the marsh smell began, the air clean enough
till we stirred up the mud, slogging through
to the blinds, our trails filling in
with a fetid thickness of oozes, only the pale
swath of bent reeds to show how we'd come.

The lake leached in from beneath. Where we walked
was something less earth than water, swelling
with bubbles that burst through the duckweed and cress,
our faces at intervals swept with clean stony gusts
from the open lake. The mallows were springy

with redwings. Everywhere flashed green bolts
of dragonflies, snakes and turtles cruised
the channels, feathers of mud braided lakeward. At dawn
came the ducks, the sky awash to the feathery roots
of its undersoils—mallard and canvasback,

teal swung in to the blinds or flared
on some sheen of the wind. In the marshes at Suamico,
watchful, we felt the world borne down
by its own abundancies. Wherever we broke
through the pursy earth there billowed about us a quick

exhalation of soils, a rich, recognizable stink,
while over us there in the dawn shone the bird-ridden sky.

—from *Cardinals in the Ice Age*, 1987

Night Bird

At moonset the stars
flung themselves apart
from one another, the frogs
which had rejoiced all night

at the river's edge fell silent,
and from the deep mulch of shadow
underneath the spruce
commenced in its turn

a night bird of some kind,
which until morning
called two hundred times
and more, though surely

it was nameless to itself.

The Naming

This is the kind of night
on which Yuan Chen cried out
to his dead wife, *when one
dreams of another, are both
aware of it?* the shadows lying close
in his bed, ice roaring
in the great river. From such a night

Adam himself awoke, knowing
none of this had ever been,
opened his eyes
onto the glorious mess of the contingent,
propped himself on one elbow,
and without astonishment gave names
to the *bee-orchid*, the *giraffe*.

—from *Vivaldi in Early Fall*, 1981

Cardinals

I saw the cardinal
from the kitchen window
on one of the first warm days—
scarlet puff at the center

of the holly bush, a red
beaked and black-eyed berry,
his crest lifted
to the wind. I tapped the glass,

but it was only when I walked out
and reached into the bush
so that I was no more
than five inches from taking him

into the circle of my thumb and finger
where I thought he might burn
like a small beating flame,
that suddenly he sleeked

and flickered low across the yard
into the heart of a dark cedar.

—from *Cardinals in the Ice Age*, 1987

Muskrat

The sky opened itself
to the dank reedy smell that was the lake
at that hour, the moon rode
in the parting of clouds
for fully a minute,
and I glanced out at the water
through the cluster of pale evening duns
on the screen, the moon-lighted dazzle
of wings, and saw

the fiery V–shape bearing out
into the shatter of light on the lake,
slow comet of small flesh
whiskery with grasses.

A small light of stars
behind the clouds, room light
behind me—in that night without true fire,
everything cold, night deepening, the lake deepening,
the deepening clarity of flight
in the wing of the imago,

I raised my arm and room light flung
the long, articulated shadows of thumb and finger
out onto the lake, out there, where
through the cold, adoptive fires
of the cold stone of the fireless moon
the muskrat swam. It was enough

to frighten him, to make him dive,
frantically, smoothly webfoot down
through the rank blacknesses of lake, his fur
trailing light, his wake starry with bubbles, his body

light with the last terrified breath-taking. He dived
into the thickening muds of the lake,
and what remained, what I was left to see,
was the floating scatter of cattails,
and how the black field of the lake
closed on his small, inexplicable fire.

—from *Vivaldi in Early Fall*, 1981

The Geese

Stepping out onto the back porch
in the early evenings of November,
I was greeted by hissing, the dumb
unfriendly voices of geese.

But in the mornings, in all the cold
decorum of light, I walked
in the crackling garden, scuffing my boots
through the frozen green hillocks of goose droppings,

shivered and watched the Toulouse geese
parading their coop roof, the goose yard
shining with spread wings. Then
night came, and the moon dimmed

in a blue web of cloud and the birches
at the yard's far edges swayed
like the white necks of geese;
and each time I felt night as a bird

and myself caught in the warm angle
between wing and body of a bird
sharing the convulsion of desire it was
to beat down on the stony planet, and rise, and fly.

—from *Vivaldi in Early Fall*, 1981

The Crows

When it was spring in Wisconsin, and the roosting crows
screamed every morning from the birches
across the lake, alarmed
by the first predatory light,

I used to push out from shore
on my little waterlogged raft
awash to my ankles, and find it possible
to believe myself standing on still water
over the dangerous place
where the sand bottom dropped
into the muds of the spring hole.

When it was spring in Wisconsin, and morning,
the nights never far away and the stars
preparing to burn in the rising field of the lake,
when it was spring and what I stood on
did not fully bear me up,
and if I could drown or fly or hurl myself
into the right and left of the powerful distances,

I had not sufficiently fathomed
how to believe, intent as I was
on the instance of morning, the voice
of the crow, small
shivers of air in the delicate drum
of the bone, the rising
beaked sun. I would stand on the lake
in the jaws of the opening light,
a deepening beneath me, a greater overhead,
the gesture of my reaching out to either side
a movement of so little extension I might,
but do not remember, have shouted
aloud and heard in reply

my own voice fly at me, back
from the trees of the far shore, the words
jumbled and raucous, prolonged
into warning, back
like the bright alarm
of the sun-greeting voices of crows.

—from *Cardinals in the Ice Age*, 1987

Snowy Owl

One day, stopping at the barn, we looked
and he was gone, and has not
to any of ten winters
journeyed back. We recollect

how everywhere about the barn the world
grew wary, quieted, and hid. But never
did we see him fly or hunt. Never
did his lonely and terrific voice

augment the neighborhood. Though overhead
had squawked and stormed a fury of crows,
he did not move or blink,
but governed there, unflawed in stillness,

except once briefly clashed
the blue hook of his beak. Oh, we
admired that wonder! But he left,
being not indigenous, and starving.

—from *Cardinals in the Ice Age*, 1987

Damselfly, Trout, Heron

The damselfly folds its wings
over its body when at rest. Captured,
it should not be killed
in cyanide, but allowed to die
slowly—then the colors,
especially the reds and blues,
will last. In the hand
the damselfly crushes easily
into a rosy slime.
Its powers of flight
are weak. The trout

feeds on the living damselfly—
the trout leaps from the water
and if there is sun you will see
the briefest shiver of gold,
then the river again.
When the trout dies
it turns its white belly
to the mirror of the sky.
The heron fishes for the trout

in the gravelly shallows on the far
side of the stream. The heron
is the exact blue of the shadows
the sun makes of trees on water.
When you hold the heron most clearly
in your eye, you are least certain
it is there. When the blue heron dies
it lies beyond reach
on the far side of the river.

—from *Weather-Fear*, 1983

Apple Trees

Among the cherry saplings in the spring
I saw the lichenous dry trunk
of the wild Spy, its one-limbed blossoming.

Then in fall
the McIntosh turned black of leaf
after one thin bearing of a dozen fruits,

and I was obliged to fell it. But in May
it sprang up in a hairy vigor of new shoots,
and I cut them back, and they

leaped up again and again, which I admired,
though I knew you would be bound to say
how neither the dying back nor the splendid

rising from the dry wood was more
than merely the dumb way of things—
which I, bound long in the orders of Desire,

would say I had understood.

—from *Cardinals in the Ice Age*, 1987

Cobra

I fear the cobra that the keeper
has teased from its box, and which has reared
and spread its hood, hissed, lunged
at the keeper's yellow boots, gathered

struck, regathered. I shudder back
from the edge of the pit, gather myself,
for though the keeper desperately has tried
to distract him, I have been singled out,

he has fixed on me, he has broken loose,
in a flash is at my feet, rising there breast-high
in the terrible display. And like no one before him
and nothing I have ever hoped to know,

is so eagerly alert to the quick
lick of my blood, that though he does not
immediately strike, I feel spread
from the clenched heart I find I have

until this moment only indeterminately borne,
a paralysis of exaltation, a long
shiver of acknowledgment so powerful
that suddenly I have found my hand

to have extended itself, to be wavering
only inches from his open jaws,
thumb and fingers fused into the glossy plates
of a snake's head, become eyed, intent, fanged,

and then lengthening into a scaled body
that unroots from my shoulder,
falls and coils, spreads the eyed hood,
rears, readies—so that there at my feet

I see them both look back
each at the dreadful other, I see
each stare both ways
in the wary, commensurate longing.

—for Julia Alvarez

—from *Cardinals in the Ice Age*, 1987

Love Poem

How definitely, for once,
he spoke! And indeed
she seemed moved, even
thoughtful—though also

she looked at him as if
he were some especially unterrifying
apparition. And when at last
they parted—oh then

he could not say he was not
without regret! In fact
at that very moment
the doors of the sky clanged thunderous

and final overhead, and night
took charge,
formal as always—but as always
quick to close everything down.

The Walled Garden

A riverbank
outside a walled garden. Later,
the interior of the garden. Later still
a rose-plot, surrounded by
a hedge, inside
the larger garden. Its single garnishment
a great sun, powerfully
shines. Unhappily

this garden is empty, although
from time to time outside the walls
a bird sings, and there occurs
a shower of warm rain. But to the north,
far to the north, it begins: snow falls,

and it is just then that from nowhere,
at the very center of the garden appears
someone who notices
the slight shortening of the days, the bare

chill of the air in the first
light of the first morning, gives way
to the first dream, sees
a scarlet sun the size of a rosebud
unfolding and unfolding from its locked center.
And when in time the first snow blows

over the walls, he makes it out to be
no more than clouds of petals
from some blooming tree. Such then

the scene and such the character
who finally sleeps and is crushed
by the great ice coming over him,
the whole time warm in the dream, the body

of the earth hollow beneath him,
and the garden no garden at all
as if it had never been
and all time spilled for nothing.

—from *Vivaldi in Early Fall*, 1981

Details of the Frozen Man

At the pole the sun circles
and circles. When at last

we raise his casket and open it
his face unclouds

from the ice—first, blue skin
of forehead, knuckles, nose tip,

then the sodden wool of the shroud,
thin shadow of red beard. Finally

he is melted free and lies
curved as a sleeping man

at rest in himself, spine flexed
and tapering to the lively

roundnesses of skull, his eyes
blue-white around the inpitched

irises, one staring as if
to recall itself, lips drawn, tongue

in the tight beam of our little light
so fixed as to seem willed

to its perfect silence. Something
soft-welling, heavy as oil, overflows

this catchment. Circling
the casket, milling about,

on the verge of ceremony, we glance
at one another and away and down

into the grave, where his hands
cross on one another

like a living man's, the nails
torn, yellow, sad.

The Guardian of the Lakes at Notre Dame

I cannot any longer bring to mind
the name of the ancient Brother
who patrolled the lakes at Notre Dame
and ran us kids off, waving his old gun
from the far shore, shouting in a voice
that from one hundred yards away
seemed dangerous as a sword.

Retired to guard the lakes, the old man did.
For him to wake up was most powerfully to insist
that turtles be troubled merely to feed,
herons to fly, snakes to dream of toads.
Himself the caring center of all careless natural grace,
at last he died. The lakes were fished.

There is perhaps something to be said
in favor of old men who raise the guardian arm and voice
against the hunting children—who, but lately come
to Paradise, pursue the precedent beast
unto its dumb destruction, and persist.

And surely the sky came more and more to seem to him
like the dark-enclosing vault of the dead box-turtle's shell.
Perhaps he thought to cry against the children was like love,
love being often in rebuke of innocence.
In all events, we plundered the far shore
and he waved his gun and shouted out at us
go home go home! in fierce stern order that we might
be made to see how in the end the bellowing angel
raises up his fist, and how that is to be
forfeit of name in the memory of men.

—from *Vivaldi in Early Fall*, 1981

Locked Out

"Why don't you call the landlord?" one of them said.
The afternoon was cold, the window ledge
just out of reach to the left, three feet away.
I had to stand precarious on the narrow rail
of the hallway balcony, back to the wall, reach out
with my left hand somehow to find a hold
among the mortar joints, and then,
hinging on hand and foot,
pivot, right leg swung out
over the yard, fingers desperate for
some catchable roughness. If
everything worked, I'd end up spraddled

in the ⊗ of the circled man—
breathing hard, hanging on to the window frame,
screwed flat to the round casement,
goggling scare-eyed through the glass
at the yellow fish that schooled
the sunny curtains of my shower stall.
I could not spare

an instant of misbalance, for the earth
awaited twenty feet below, disguised as a layer
of crumbling concrete, the floor
of the courtyard oozing and pooled,
trash in its corners. I faltered
on the rail. I needed more courage
than ever I had. Next door

the gardener leaned on his rake and stared.
The mail man, fanning a sheaf
of yellow envelopes, craned for a clearer look,
while from the kitchen door directly underneath,
the landlord's cook stepped out to shade
his eyes at me, and stood
foreshortened, arms erupting
from his ears, feet in white sneakers
fringing his chin. I stretched
and reached and inched along a bit,
fearful and overbalanced. I could barely touch
the window frame. Some one of the watchers said,
"You're going to kill yourself!" Another said
"Get a ladder." I hadn't thought of that.

"Or a locksmith." Nor of that.
"You're going to kill yourself."
Inside where I could not see
dwelt his shadowed, breathable air. Books trembled
along his mantelpiece, eggs dreamed
in the fridge. Everything slept silent
in its chartered place. I wavered there.
Inside his rooms a silence grew

and grew; I had the sense it might accumulate
so greatly as to burst the door,
like a powerful wind boil down the corridor
and tear me from my holds. Locked out,
ready to fall, I shouted down at them, at all
the watchers, to whichever one, *"As for
the landlord, he's never to be found!"*

Falling on Blood Mountain

You slip in the talus
of the lower trail, and bruise
the heel of your palm,

and even if it does not show,
the rock you stopped yourself against
is itself deeply broken,

the shock of your fall
having unfolded into the root
of Blood Mountain, then

deeper. Someone
on the other side of the earth
awakens and wonders why,

and falls back. Meanwhile
the blood darkly congeals
in the pulsing root of your hand.

—from *Blood Mountain*, 1977

Sister Vincent

Sister Vincent couldn't pray,
and so required us every day
to pray for her. In every prayer
we never doubted our despair.

She bribed me once with apple tart
to quicksilver her Sacred Heart,
and wore it blazing on her gown
until in time it tarnished brown,

and she grew stern, and red of eye
but did not weep—I wondered why,
and wonder still. She'd paid me well
to wear the brightest heart in Hell.

Grown old and somewhat stout,
Sister Vincent went in doubt,
once she'd found the heart could dull
and apples thunder in the skull.

Sister Vincent tried to pray
but died still mute one holiday.
I have not prayed since I was young
but tasted apples on the tongue.

—from *The Homer Mitchell Place*, 1968

Clearing

One day walking together
careless beneath the refractive canopy
of the October woods,
we were stopped, hurled back

by solid light, our minds,
unready, flung
to the clearing's farther edge.
There we turned,

looked back to see
across a barren of ferns
our empty bodies, lost,
bewildered, sick with ignorance

and fear—but light
intervened. Up
from the saturate heart of the earth
it sprang and flooded

sulfurous in the living woods.
Everywhere about us bled
the raw, seasonal edges.
There we stood.

—from *Cardinals in the Ice Age*, 1987

At Night on the Lake in the Eye of the Hunter

That night, drifting far out
in the center of the lake,
I watched the stars; later
I shone my torch down into the eel grass
of the perch beds and saw the fish
stunned into thrills and tremblings of fins.

I shone the torch onto my wet hands,
the wet sky-reflecting floorboards
of the boat, onto the sky itself,
the beam widening and thinning into the white
fabrics of mist. That night

I thought I rode the center of all
the widening brightnesses
to the rimstones of the encircling earth.
Later by starlight seeing
over the whole blue surface of the lake
trout feeding on mayflies,
seeing the cross and recross
of rise rings, the slow
opening ripples
from the tiny bright insucks
at center,

I came to think how it might have been
my boat hung there in a net of light,
a cold, translatable fire.
However it was, the light began

its long reach, even now,
long afterward, still
rising, widening into the body of the sky,
into the last huge widenesses of the last
meetings of light beyond which I remember this
or not, beyond which
even then fearing my life
I wished to burn.

—from *Vivaldi in Early Fall*, 1981

The Raft

His father told him to be careful,
to go no farther than the boundaries
of the lily cove. His father told him
once more about his cousin Archie

who had fallen into the scalding water
of the switchyard sump because
the cinders floating there between the tracks
had made it seem to be dry ground.

"He wasn't thinking where he was.
He wasn't watching, he was thinking
of something else," his father said.
So he agreed that he would watch

where he was going, wanting badly
to get down to the lake and out
to where he couldn't see
the bottom, to where

it would not be evidently safe. "That day
he never came home to eat, he never
came home, he was dead, and nobody
knew, they just

went on with whatever it was
they were doing for themselves!" His father
was going on and on like that
when he ran out the door and down

to the old dock and found the raft
hidden in the reeds along the shore,
splintery pine boards scummy
with mud and moss; and when

he pushed it into the knee-deep water
at the end of the dock, and stood, it ducked
and wavered and nearly heaved him off,
but held, an inch awash, instep-deep.

He sprawled down onto his belly
and paddled out with his hands,
like swimming—from the house
his father might have seen him

confidently swimming, headed out beyond
the boundaries, but in fact safe,
even should he range beyond the cove
to the dark line where the wind began—

though it was strange, even fearful,
to cup his hand around his eyes, lean
close to the surface so that his nose
touched water, and look

through water and see
dense golden fields of weed. It was strange
to want so much to stand up on the raft,
step boldly off and walk

over the feathery tips of the weeds
to shore, his father watching, walk
straight up on shore and call
to the terrified house

that he was safe, and had come back, and the lake
had held up as he had known it would
and there had been from the first nothing
to worry about, nothing at all.

Staring down into the water, still bellied
into the raft, he saw
the skin of the lake thicken
with fiery clouds because the sky

had thickened with fiery clouds
so that there in the blazing lake,
in the pale cloud of his unwary face,
was the awful issue of the looking back.

—from *Cardinals in the Ice Age*, 1987

The Photograph

From the young birch lining the far shore
the crows called, erupted into the sky
out of the yellow leaves, flurried there,
fell back. The sun was high,

everything in perfect order on the raft,
the anchor rope in a tight spiral, weighed
by the scarlet coffee can half-filled
with cedar-smelling loam

from the swamp's edge. He spilled
a handful onto the rough pine
of the deck, threaded a worm, and let it down,
careful it didn't snag, until the line

went slack, and he thought the lead
might have touched bottom, drew it up a bit,
then waited, leaning over, trying to see
into the shadows among the twists

of pickerel weed, the light
where it touched the water going green,
slanting down into the weed beds, silvery
with water dusts and pollens. Over the clean

sand bottom schools of yellow perch,
bluegills, redeyes, lavender and flash
of shiners, waver and ripple of light,
short bursts of gold and green

where the young bass fed. But nothing
happened, nothing. He waited for a fish,
and when he looked up, his eyes
dazzled at the sky. It was as if he still

were looking into the water, for the sun
was low, and a green light rose
from the cedars. His mother stood
on the beach and called, but he chose

not to hear, though she called and called.
At last he looked up and saw her there
farther off than he had thought
her dress blowing, her feet in deep sand.

So he began to paddle back, the raft
wanting to turn in circles, the wind
opposing him. So he stood and leaned
into his paddle, dug hard, looked up again

and the beach was empty, the lake
ruffling, the water going dense
and steely. It took him more time
than he'd thought he had to get back. It was not

as if he'd truly had a choice—the wind
had turned against him, and when
he stared into the water his face
did not look back. He felt the rain begin,

and while he struggled toward the beach
his mother came back and took a photograph
that caught the raft low down in the chop
seeming a powerful distance from shore,

and him, paddle in hand, the birch
on the far shore bristling up from the snowy sand,
everything badly overexposed—it frightened him to see
how far out on the lake he'd been.

He was frightened not to see
his face, but only a dark shape
under the hat brim. Even though
it had been in Klondike in the general store

where he'd stood to hold and see the photograph,
under his feet the plank floor dry
and gritty, it hadn't been at all
certain that the foolish one in the photograph

was not slowly sinking into the dark lake, endangered
and alone, calling out to the mother who stood intent
her camera to her eye, framing him there,
catching the birches, the crows overhead,

the lake rising on him—somehow the fishy air
gathering, the sky gathering, around him
the deepening smell of cedar before rain,
the blue surge of lightning for the instant withheld.

—from *Cardinals in the Ice Age*, 1987

Turtle Hunter

Fingers and forearms terrified and chill,
I grabbled blind in the murky water
for the sawtooth edges of carapace,

caught desperate hold, tussled and flung
into the boat the raging snapper I'd trod up
from the cobbled bottom, scabrous,

spraddled and pissing, stony jaws
agape, plastron a fringe of leeches,
the one stone that of all

the dark-enclosing others had humped
under my foot, in the dangerous throb
of startlement thrust back.

When in Wisconsin

When in Wisconsin where I once had time
the flyway swans came whistling in
to the rotten Green Bay ice, and stayed
not feeding, four days, maybe five,

I shouted and threw stones to see them fly.
Blue herons followed—or came first.
I shot a bittern's wing off with my gun.
For that my wife could cry.

My neighbor's wife mistook the spawning frogs
for wood ducks nesting the white pines
up on Bean Hill—I straightway set her right.
Each April during rainy nights

I lantern-hunted for salamanders
where they hid toe-walking the bottom
mucks and muds. I shuddered
at the scored skin of their sides, the deep

flesh tucks. In hand, they dried. I waded
through frog spawn. Once I'd hoped
the great white birds might brake
for the frog ditch, and alight—

but now the addled past collapses on itself,
splash rings close inward on the rising stone,
the gun sucks fire, bone becomes
whole bone, light narrows back

on filament and point, the forest turns
to sand, and only season lacking source
rolls round and round until in my turns I fall
forever back, clutching my stone, my gun, my light.

—from *Signals From the Safety Coffin*, 1975

Feeding the Swans

Far across the lake we saw through snow
shadows of mountains. Nearer
milled rafts of canvasback, flaring

and edgy at dusk. Our buckets empty
we turned home whereupon
the three swans, cygnet, cob and pen,

that had hung offshore as long as we stood there
came wary up the beach to feed.
With what elegant hesitation

they'd refused us as we tried
to lure them in, handful by handful
broadcasting on the sand

the yellow corn, yet failed—
meantime, the first skin
of the first ice edging in.

—for Vince and Betty

Terribilis est locus iste

I recall
that when I held the leghorn
upside down, her head—
lemony beak gaping and crooning—
swiveled to fix in its balances
craned calmly to see until

I lopped it away on the chopping block
and she ran to flap in the pit
of the cold-frame among
the seedling kohlrabi, the cut neck skin
pursed on its raw stem. I recall

how I would stand to watch,
how sufficiently convinced
of bird fury and din
in the wholly silent yard,

the day bright and the sun fixed
among soft feathers of cloud,
but only my brain
in its dreadful balances squawked
and screamed and lay down
in the delicate tremor.

Today the sun drains downwards
in red trails, the sun
like an owl's eye swells,
and I listen, I hear
the burgeoning tumor
that will measure me. Was it the moon

in silence rising before me
through all the colors of brass?
Was it the sun or the moon?

In the petals of the great fire,
in the radiant gold of its ash
I tasted my tongue, I saw
the gasping still recognizable
skull, I was crowded
with flowers and leaves. This

is no age of faith, rats
gnaw at the holy paste, and we
lie down in the ultimate tremor,
the delicate blood spray
brightening on leaves—though it has been
the simplest dying, the cleanest

of butcheries, this
is a dreadful place, it is
the House of God, the Gate
of Heaven—I am appalled
by these uproars of the blood, I regard

the hen's foot clenched
and drowned in its yellow broth,
her cleaned thighbones agleam
among the crumbs of the dumplings.

—from *Signals From the Safety Coffin*, 1975

Olduvai

Glance down at your feet
stop, kneel and scrape
with bare fingers in the red, abrasive soils

until it is loosened from the matrix,
then take it up, hold it, smooth
the polished vault, peer close

at the astonishing checks and crazings, pause
for a good while,
little dry cascades

of red earth dribbling
from every aperture—*skull!*
skull! Look up. Everything

will have changed, except
for the faint, diminishing
heart's aftershock.

In Cedar Grove Cemetery

all summer I followed the curves
of the black path beyond
the buckeye grove and past
the Founder's plot, until

in the west back corner beside
the golf course fence, next
to the stone with the oval
photograph of John Rybicki
I found the old depression

of the child's grave, lay down,
fitted myself into its shallow
giving-way, on my belly
in prairie grasses, peered
through thatches

of wild rose, my fingers
in cow vetch. I smelled
the summer smell, fat green
of crushed grass, and something
dark, like roots. Deep

in Cedar Grove the big trees leaned
to the wind, horse chestnuts boomed
on the gravestones. I nested there
to watch the golfers lining up their putts,
and afterwards reach in

to retrieve the balls, their hands
to the wrists in the green. At times
I made it out to be
they were pausing, fumbling,
stumbling back as if

terrified, seeming to brace
and pull back, as if
something inches below the grass
had caught at their fingers, as if before
my very eyes I had seen

the blunt tooth of the earth
take hold, and the feeding begin,
the dogged, voluptuous swallowing.

Beans

Bean vines leap half up their trellises
nearly to blind the window,
and in no more than a week

obscure the view,
sun and moon, yard
and currant hedges, roses,
gooseberries, the spruce

beneath which the house dogs
vigorously sleep, above all
the fiery mountain
above the tides of shadow,

in the certain imperfection
of the future everything
lost to view,
to my true knowledge

nightly eroded
wholly beyond repair.
At voiceless midday
the sun stalls

and over everything
wavers a salty stink
like mud flats and because
I greatly wish it,

outside ought to be shining
the ocean. Instead
the light is no more than sun
through the translucent leaves

of the young bean plants,
the smell no more
than my own sweat, well on its way
to considerably worse than sour.

—for Alenka Rainer

Bog Plants

Thirteen years later the night is the purple flush
of the pitcher plant's throat. Sitting alone,
the beginning of error, I think
of the flower, the snake-mottled
belly of leaf that bulged from the loam near the hose;
and the clawed pads of the flytrap, that never mistook
my probing with straws for the brunt
of the entering beetle, the sundews I moved
from the Berrien bogs to grow
in the house's north shade,
in late June, in those days when the skies
over South Bend were burning, burning,
and if there was rain, it came down as a power of light.

I remember the light—as my eye today
unfocuses, suffers no clarity, then
it blurred and recoiled from the sun on the white
east side of the house, the house giving back
such dazes of light, so blinding, I turned
to stare into the shades of the ell, the damp
corner of bog plants, the blindness
come over me, consequent
nightmare—

        my body at rest in the white, cool soils of the bed,
my head foursquare on the pillow, the sheets
so neat at my chin that merely to stir
was to trouble the whole
house and its bordering acres,
I dreamed I was thorax of wasp, the impervious
chitins of beetle, carapace, husk
a blurring, corrodable heart,
the bone sour in the belly's
vigorous juices. And there was the slow
large, convulsive gulp of the dark.

—from Vivaldi in Early Fall, 1981

Bullhead

Sprawled belly-down on the damp planks,
the breath squeezed in my chest,
I drift the bait into the pale
moon-shadow of the dock

waiting for the blunt
emergence of bullhead, his slow
surge at the worm, glint
of the small mucusoid eye—
sluggish black spasm of flesh.

He bites, and I haul him out,
but he does not die at once—
ugly among fish, poisonous dorsal spine erect,
he endures, he swims in the air
for hours, scrabbles and grunts
in the bucket. A hundred times I have heard

that gross croaking from the bucket,
and it comes to the memory
from that peculiar sleeplessness
which loves those things which resemble

other things—night
after night I have tried
to breathe the inappropriate air,
wanted to cry out
into the blackness beyond
the dumb immediate blackness

that I am about to die and cannot die,
but have made so dull a voice of the dull
connatural agony I've writhed to it,
grunting aloud, the hook
of the breath snagged
in my gullet, the tongue
in my mouth like a worm.

—from *Cardinals in the Ice Age*, 1987

The Fish Dream

In Bikini when as sudden
as the mirror of a wing
light came, the wind changed,

and hot dust mucked
our crannies up,
we locked ourselves below,

turned off the air, and stack gas
boiled in the passageways. Topside
the flight deck bloomed

with a thousand fountains,
and below decks six times a day
we showered in salt water

and held our breaths. Later
we lay like stains
in the sodden bunks

and it made for dreams—umber-
scaled and yellow-spotted fish
with six-inch needle teeth

crept out on fleshy fins over
the blazing decks and gorged our heads
while we stared on, afraid to wake.

—from *Signals From the Safety Coffin*, 1975

Hagfish

Behold the swimmer, afloat between
a staring sun and the dim oozes:
he gazes down through a lustrous sea
which, as it deepens, closes

on its green light. His shadow might be
a wreck, or a deep reef. All at once he feels
the soft blow at his groin, cruel rasp
of jaws, long slither of entry.

He is frightened, loses strength,
declines to the peaceful sea bed
where there is light enough so that
when in green murk he half awakes

he cannot keep himself from the sight
of the bulging wound from out of which
powerfully prolongs itself that length
of ropy body, the blind head, and working jaws.

Clearly it has not been a mere
unhappy dreaming that the swimmer
should have felt that strange
surge in his belly, knot and odd

emptying at heart. Now he lies helpless
in a place he knows nothing about.
He does not wish to give up
what he feels slipping away.

This is the fate he has expected,
and managed thus far to escape.
But he has been unwary,
and without warning he is inhabited,

the inhabitation is complete. Light
will never brighten or deaden
more than this. Above, at its great depth,
the surface softly glitters.

Pigeons

I don't love the fat rabble of pigeons
that from my first day in this place
has swarmed gluttonous from distant neighborhoods
at dawn and dusk, hooting and babbling, shitting
the yard, the eaves, smothering
the few green spasms of new grass. And this morning

for the third day in a row they
wake me up, fluting at dawn from the ridgepole,
scratching at the roof slates, rousing me to fly
enraged to the window to terrify them off
with shout, handclap, window-bang—upon which

they flurry and burst from the filthy ledges,
each time—I admit it—beautifully,
as if a hundred silvery shards of roof
have in an irregular wind torn loose, feathered risen.
But scared to merely one orbit of the neighborhood,
each time increased in number, they return, stall

over the house, descend, immense
filthy fluttering, greedy seethe of wings,
derangement of green and coral
iridescences, and in less than a minute

have overrun the feeder, that on our first day
in this new place I planted
at the center of its treeless, birdless,
gardenless back yard.

Cardinals in the Ice Age

When Louise called to tell me
a pair of cardinals was at her feeder
and had been around for days,
I was, besides envious, reassured,

not having at my own tray seen
a cardinal in years. I had grown in fact
to fear I might not soon again.
I had thought they must have fled

the growing inclemencies of this place
to somewhere farther south and it was clear
I lacked the strategies to lure them north
again. To me this was in the way of a most

considerable loss. But here were cardinals,
or word of them, and any time I chose
I might cross the road and see them for myself—
and yet stayed home, for while it was a short walk,

the day was cold, the road a difficult course
of icy ruts, and they were not my cardinals
but Louise's. Besides, wasn't it enough to know
the birds were back, there in my neighbor's yard,

bright on the vivid snow? I took this
to be rare and necessary evidence that still
some time remained before the first lobes
of the great oncoming ice on its long probe south

awakened the neighborhood one night
to the sounds of our mountains going down,
screech of rock on bedrock, huge
morainal wave of houses, boulders, trees,

and finally a dull moon reflecting
from the still face of the ice cliff
looming two miles overhead
into a birdless sky.

—from *Cardinals in the Ice Age*, 1987

Traveling

Afraid, I was always afraid:
we would be late, our seats
stolen, that once aboard

in the close compartments
someone would light up, and then
should I object, in anger

and contempt he would rebuke me,
that on hot days
someone would require the windows

to be closed, play music
too loud, pretend
to not understand when I inquired

where we might be, how far
we might have come, where
we were bound, had yet

to go; that ours
might be the wrong train
through inattention

wrongly boarded, and we
were lost, irretrievable,
unticketed; that we

had long passed and repassed
our destination, that the intolerable
delays on the dark sidings

required firm looking into, though
to whom I ought to address myself,
according to what stance and tone

I did not know, and so continued
restless, weary and impatient;
that there had slipped my mind

that which I from the very first
was cautious to remember; that outside
were truly nothing

but dull fields, smoke,
black snow; that it was certain we
had been re-routed, given

no notice, would not
arrive, and should have
hours ago.

—from *Cardinals in the Ice Age*, 1987

Prince Mahasattva on Blood Mountain

Where the forest grows
to the very edge of the precipice
on Blood Mountain, I see

Prince Mahasattva remove
his crimson robe, and hang it
on leafless branch. I see him leap

from the precipice. His sash
trails behind him, a delicate
twisted flame. Below, in the valley,

a starving tigress with her seven cubs
is waiting. About the head and body
of Prince Mahasattva are flowers

like birds, or birds
like flowers. The tigress
watches the body of Prince Mahasattva

in flight. His body arches
like a bent bow. His eyes close.
He reaches out with his hands

for the waiting beast,
or he is praying,
or both.

—from *Blood Mountain*, 1977

With Zimmer at the Zoo

From the very outset
we'd thought we would be late,
from the very first

thought the zoo would soon
be closing, when in truth
it barely had opened, then

through an entire morning
did nothing but stare
at the bull giraffe in his slow

floating run about the moated
enclosure. About noon
a bellowing and caterwaul

arose from the far side of the park
from what must have been
a fierce, considerable beast—

the truth was
the singular animals we were keen to see
were but recently removed

from exhibition, and in
their expensive compounds slept,
and would not be awakened. The truth was,

we would not in the short remainders of our lives
have opportunity to pass this way again
and feared that in our final hours

we'd dream how just at closing
had we possessed courage
and the art, we might

have slipped inside, evaded
the keepers till deep at night
when the zoo awoke to roar its great

and varied chorus to the moon, then stood
close by the shining fence, and loud
in our solitudes, mooed with the Bongo.

Silent Film

We come around a sharp bend in the road
   and there unbalanced on the top rung of a ladder,
arms flailing, stands a man
    with a comic mustache,
     while from the open window strains to him
       a girl most delicate, hands clasped
at her right ear, bright hair unbound, her bosom
heaving and her eyes cast up
for the help that is certain not to come.

      Another man, the father in his outrage,
braces himself akimbo at the ladder's foot,
   stroke upon stroke lopping it away
        until, still climbing and intent,
         the suitor stands upon the ground

ankle-deep in splinters, whereupon
  he pauses uncertain, bewilderedly aware
  something is not right, and just in time

  leaps to the bright sweep of the blade,
   then disappears at double speed
      around the corner of the house, knees high
and pumping, the terrible parent
  hot on his heels, the girl
in the last and bitter sag of her defeat,
      fallen out of sight. Neither of us
  finds it necessary to restrain
the other, the thing is concluded, no use
  to interfere. And so together
   we wander off, each
      uncertain whether he has not
    discerned within himself some small
        ignobility of sentiment before
  the sorry spectacle. Each knows in the other
singular capacity for Love,
  for Pity and Desire, likewise
  for Righteousness, but also

the clownish hitch
    in the fundamental plasms . . . therefore
will neither of us
    risk ourselves outright to laugh.

                              —for David Huddle

The Waiters at The Park Hotel, Belgrade

were unavailable, however urgently
we called out to them, beckoned, displayed
irritation. Their backs

turned, they paid us
no mind, never spoke, but again
and again, flushed

and cursing, hurled themselves
into the infernal kitchens, returning
spent, to brood over the bitter

aperitifs, the very
and fragrant coffees, breads,
rich soups for which,

before the chill import of their disdain,
the icy choirs of their plates
and linens, lustres

of cutlery, stern shinings
of crystal, we suffered ourselves
powerfully to hunger.

—for Katha Pollitt, September 1985

The Hunters

Traveling, our plans in ruin
by reason of an unseasonable snow,
the day gone sour with the silences we kept,
through the dark afternoon impatient

for the Belgrade train, we waited
in the bitter restaurant
of the Vojvodina Hotel, dispossessed
of our poor room

to accommodate the Italian hunters
who one table away complained
about the dogs, their guides,
our room, the moldy bread, a cup

with a chipped lip—or so Miša in scorn
translated for us, saying it was
normal, this was the way
in this place at this hotel

this time of the year that anyone
ought to have expected it to be.
But we had not so expected it to be,
for oh but the yellow grease congealed

on the chill, unhappy restaurant plates,
upstairs sat empty our room we could not use,
and all the while far out on the foggy plain
pheasants preened and crowed and crowded

in the stubbles of the maize fields, hares
played in multitudes beyond imagining,
roebuck bellowed and leaped at the forest's edge
in herds, in herds! Everywhere

browsed and rooted deer and boar, the marshes
were raucous with geese, big pike
and carp threshed the shallows
into foam. Had we the inclination,

we could fish and hunt.
But we were cold and tired,
and yearned for sleep. Besides,
against the restaurant windows rained a slush

of snow and fog and coal smoke. Our weapons
lay disassembled in their sleeves.
And whatever remained of the light, it did not count.

—from Cardinals in the Ice Age, 1987

Taxi

From over our cabby's shoulder
in the rear-view mirror I observed
the angry driver of the scarlet Zastava
with both hands rend his head, and lean

raging into the windshield. Traffic was hot
and solid to either side, and close
the red car followed, swerving,
desperate to pass. Our driver, loud

in his power, sang joyful to the radio,
and we—we huddled, certain we would die,
and begged to slow him down, but lacked
syntax. So there we were,

hurtling terrified along
the very center line
of Marsala Tita, and God knew
what lay ahead. Once I thought

to leap the seat and wrest the wheel away,
but saw that then we were the more
inevitably doomed, being travelers, strangers, lost
and insufficient, unable with clarity

to see enough ahead
to mark the proper turnings
and prepare for them.

—from *Cardinals in the Ice Age*, 1987

Shark

I step into this memory
a foot from myself, a road
diminishing behind, and ahead
Marseilles. I'm walking back
from somewhere in late afternoon,

the sea blue as a flax field to my left,
a hill strangled with vetch
to my right, bright orange soils
underfoot, over it
this same sky, everything

calm, blue, hot,
the earth soaking up shadows,
so it's all I can do
to keep my own shadow walking
before me into Marseilles, at last
to stretch itself out
over the foul, iridescent scums

of the harbor with its turnings
and scatters of baitfish, the sun
in billions flung back. And then

beneath it all, something
much larger, a slow
closing in from the sea, a cloud's
shadow, had the sky not been clear—then

the green milky stare of that eye
looking up at me through
the insane skitter and dash
of the bait fish into the calm
power of the day where I,
having myself but this moment arrived,

stare back through my shadow
into the harbor at the long
fish-shape of the darkness, and breathe
in no hurry at all.

Dead Pig

Not drunk, but sick
from bad fish or fowl or some
several other possibilities, in fact
almost to dying on the landing

in Marseilles, the liberty boat
long gone, the carrier
an occasional shudder
of green running light far
to sea, the sea between us
a shoaling of whitecaps
otherwise stormy with darkness,

desperate, I found a hotel
and to the night clerk tried
to explain, and say my name,
and failed, but he gave me a room,
and just barely inside, the door
still clicking shut, fallen
helpless to hands and knees,
I spewed out
everything, everywhere, onto

the floor, into bidet, toilet bowl,
sink, potted fern, then fell
on my face somewhere, half
underneath the bed, slept there until,
cheek and hair crusted
to the dusty rug, bitter-mouthed I woke
in a sour, webby light that could have been
morning, early evening, any time

of a bad day, brown
clouds, a brown sea
spitting phlegmy spray. The carrier
hours out of sight, I anyway
came down to the empty slip
and hung around awhile, nobody
to see me or ask
why I was there. Birds screamed
everywhere. I let it sink in
that the ship had sailed

without me, and there
I was, not sure
exactly where I was, but pretty sure
they'd hang me once
I got back, if I did, for how

could I explain, and who
would want to listen,
or, listening, take my word? Once

glanced into an angle of the pilings,
saw there richnesses of trash: oil sheen, clots
of fish guts, tar balls, churnings
of orange peels, turds, condoms,
then abruptly recognized
beneath the flash and swerve
of schooling alewives the delicate

pale wavering of drowned flesh,
sat up, said on the instant to myself
"Dead pig!" just like that, just that
clear-sighted, that
definite—even though

I was in plenty enough
of trouble, AWOL
and fugitive and still
a little sick, even though

the corpse was headless,
bloodless, so long awash
as to be not much more finely dense
than the harbor water, said
triumphant and aloud, *"Dead pig!"*

Walking to Cootehill

It has been a long walk to Cootehill
and back again, heel and big toe
blistered, the traffic both ways impetuous
along the narrow lanes.
For a mile or more the journey

stank of ditches, at one point
of a sheep's carcass, three weeks
powerfully dead, already on the way
to almost bones. In Cootehill

at Paddy Boyles's Mens' and Boys'
I purchased for its jauntiness
a new cap, gray wool houndstooth foxhunter,
and on the way back,

in one field spotted an old ram
dangling a hoof. Moved on his account,
I shouted to the farmer, who,
beating dust from his cap against his leg
and wiring shut the gate,
threw over his shoulder *tis only*

a thorn, no more'n a fookin thorn!
making it clear
he believed I had reproved him,
and coming back a little way

let me know I was less by far
than halfway from Cootehill, hinting

I was maybe even losing ground.
Behind me, the lane narrowed
onto distances from which diminished
the monotonous, pained bleatings
of the ram. Whitethorn and wild roses

were in raucous bloom. From everywhere
in the hedges came great chirrupings
and bustle of chaffinches,
cattle lowed, the sky
sputtered with light. I limped
along the dwindling lane, wary

of cars, suspicious
of the ditches out of which
some skittish creature, the instant
I least expected it, likely
would flush—as on my way
doves had erupted in wild flight,
hares skidded
on the macadam, and from deep
in the roadside skullcap had come
little angular breakneck skitterings. Now,

at last safely back, and wearing
this new cap, I posture where
my images converge between
the four mirrors of the Music Room,
before and behind and to either hand
grinning and scowling, cocking
the cap over one eye, then the other, alert
for the least anterior glint
of bald spot—in fact, I look,

wearing this cap, my age,
and consider returning it; in fact
I so greatly fail to be pleased
that it rockets up on garish exhausts

of question marks, exclamation points,
asterisks, arrows, stars,
to shudder, hover and bare
to the general mockery
my unbecoming skull.

—Annaghmakerrig, August 1990

Picnic

That night the sky
had brightened with a storm
no one expected, but at dawn
it grew dark. Everyone had sat

in rows on long benches in the park
at the edge of the river, the tall
grandfather, fingers thrust
through the gills of a large carp

held aloft for the photographer
to admire, the grandmother, younger
than anyone living could remember her
to have been, children, aunts, uncles

in shawls, a dog, a pet crow
on a pony's back. Patches of damp
spread on the women's skirts,
not a shadow was cast, and every object

shone with some manner of light.
How they assumed their lives! the brim
of the old man's hat blew back, his beard
ruffled, her skirt ballooned

a little in the wind. By now
they have forgotten the light, the river,
the occasion, each other, everything.
Had I known them

they would have forgotten me as well,
and I would have lost
even that small store of breath.
For I would have come upon them

unexpected, as they arranged themselves
on the benches by the Danube
and stiffened into the required poses,
no place in that close order, and no time

to spare a traveler, a stranger at that,
requiring direction, lost
and strangely grateful for his need,
but lacking the tongue,

and though inclined to fail
at the most familiar truth, stubborn
in the manner of travelers
to discern and name it—moreover ready

in his abominable accent to persist.

—from *Cardinals in the Ice Age*, 1987

Winter Flight

1

Just now, here on the runway at Milwaukee
already three hours late into Ontario
by way of Denver which is filled
beyond all possibility with snow,

my invalid father, who has always feared
to fly, comes back just long enough
to ask me, who is shepherding him west,
Are we airborne? an hour yet from taking off,

and he the whole time here beside me
so far as I can tell, half-dead,
mouth agape, a dark stain down
one trouser leg, eyes rolled into his head,

asking so as to display some shape
of interest, staring out the window
into the garish nightmare of blue runway lights
each in its pool of blue snow, that snow-

flood in a cold place neither of us
is likely to see again, nor cares to see—
then, sagging back into his seat on the dead
leg, dead arm, sour smell of the old meat

giving way, asks *How high are we?*
goes still, tries himself once hard to shove
himself upright, and fails. And I cannot help or speak
for being one who, wishing to move, moves.

2

In the thrust and vigorous angle
of the aircraft when at last
it rises, and we enter the black sky
of winter that arcs from here and west

and east of here to as far as we might
in order of safety wish to go—when
at last it rises, piercing the night clouds,
entering the watery currents of the high wind,

it is as he has been promised he should fear:
earth-pull as he could never have
imagined it, stony masses of the continent,
power of water calling after him *come back!*

flesh of belly, breasts and balls
hauled at, even the smallest
of his small bloods hauled at,
and in tumult to the east and west

the great seas he has never seen
about to spill out over the cold land,
below him the angry shallows of the lakes,
below him the forests of Wisconsin

lashing away and ahead the mountains
in sharp wait rising and hardening, ahead
and beneath him nothing with much
in the way of promise to it. Half-dead

he is for the first time flying
and the last, over the calm flowering
of the moonlit clouds, torn loose
from the entire beloved matter of things,

moving himself to move, fearing it is
in any but the most formal of descents
nothing but annihilation, flesh strewn
about the icy fields of the blue-lit planet,

which, as it turns out, falls away,
thrusts up, billows with snow and salt, surges
together, calls after him, boils up
at its ravenous verges.

—from *Cardinals in the Ice Age*, 1987

The Planet

Through binoculars last night, my arm
braced on the porch stanchion, I saw
from Long Point over the aura of Portland
bright Jupiter, and just below

the cold light of Venus. Brilliant,
the images wavered, yet clear at first
as otherwise and elsewhere the world
did not seem clear, nor the sky

above the world—two little moons
to my east of the planet, or three, the huge
discrete motions of the body
frozen there, nothing moving except

by blood tremor my hand shook so
over that time of distance that the small
trembling magnified itself, and the planet
danced and nothing

would submit itself to focus.

—from *Cardinals in the Ice Age*, 1987

At Dawn on Gun Point

I wake with a great start. I've overslept.
I haven't dreamed. I've seen the sky
coldly rejoin the horizon.
I've seen the dawn erupt

from the chill soils of the sea,
and the big oak black
with roosting crows—it's seemed
a mighty formulation of rebuke,

for certain nothing in the way
of an answering love. I'd thought
there must be things
one is required to forget.

Proofs of the Withholding

Down on the shore
big black-winged gulls
slide in from nowhere
to swarm the bluefish guts
I've just flung onto the rocks,
gasp and mutter, feeding—
and together with the onshore wind

and the small surf make another voice,
the only fit name for which I can find
is laughter. And though it's early,
the sun risen barely clear of itself,

there's all this young light on the verge of fire,
sea and sky reflected, imagined
and reimagined each
in the other so powerfully I almost doubt
the prospect of darknesses

to follow, and go on trying to look
to where the sea has become
not clearly itself,
to where it continually vanishes
past the black headland.

The Storm

I will myself not to despair
when I wait by the sea for good weather.
Even on the brightest of days
the storm has been a continual
awful hanging in the air,
and comes often, and endures,
longer each time, sometimes early
after a windless night that has been calm
with moon and stars, a fog
hanging close into the coast, soft
against the window, then
clearing, then

a line of big thunderheads advancing
from the north where last time
I happened to look nothing was, only
the broadest of daylight. And then
the sky breathes deeply,
and before I can think

the whirligig in the yard has spun itself
to pieces, the sea is shuddering to its floor,
and the sea has swelled almost window-high,
has flung itself at the window,
the window has bulged inward
and the beach plum and the beach roses
have blown flat and seem about
to uproot and fly away,

and it is here just at this spot
where America stops
thirty feet over the long unhappy reach
of the ripped sea, that this is being
written—in Maine
looking north from a streaked window
toward some black savage rock of an island
I have never seen before and that I swear

wasn't there before,
and that seems at this very instant
to have at once fallen from the sky and boiled up
from below, and is being devoured
by its surf, and can be reached
only by swimming.

THE UNNAMING

Aurora

I climbed Ledge Road on up to Prospect Street
from which I planned to look out across the lake,
over which the night before occurred
the red aurora I failed to see. I was cautious,

fearing the dull ache in my chest and arm
that warn me when I've climbed too fast,
but soon enough reached the top where
only days ago snow brooded, and while I slept

unrecollectably dreaming,
out of cold silence arose showers,
veils, fountains of red light—
never mind that next morning

the road sign cautioned that at the slow,
dangerous dip of Prospect might linger ice.

—for Richard Dillard

Comet

In 1910 when I was eight
mother took me from my bed and out
into the yard and pointed and there
over our house it shone, higher

than the chestnuts. It streamed
and billowed light, in the sky
terrible as an angel of God hovering,
about to stoop

trailing long hair and robes of fire.
I was only eight and felt terrified
to see that sight, and privileged
and never have

forgotten it. None of us
out on the lawn that night
with everything else just the way
it had always been—the tree frog

that sounded like a small bird dreaming
peeping away in the low crotch
of the chestnut, the drone
of crickets, across the street

somebody hunting night crawlers,
his lantern moving slow
along the edges of the flower beds,
the scarlet or yellow of a tulip

flashing out of the dark from time to time—
none of us knew just how
to take it. Even today, talking it over,
we're still not sure we could have seen

a thing like that, though our minds
are clear, and we remember it
as if it had been the night before. And that's
not all. Early next morning

the yard still dark, from the holly bush
a cardinal was singing, and from
the hickory a mockingbird,
and for a minute there, not quite

over the line to wakefulness
and probably by what I'd seen
still blinded to the usual ways of things,
I thought the trees

were singing. In my life
have not been many times like that one—first
a huge firework in the sky, a slow explosion
that stayed alight, then trees

singing. But soon enough
I was awake, and knew better,
and for years
have known better. For years, until just now,

the comet has held
that other recollection down.
I don't know why
it should come back to me at all,

for of that night I can't recall
anything of any person there,
not even of my mother, who held me
and spoke low, not how

she looked or what
her voice was like, or her words, it was
so long ago. Probably
I used the dream of trees

to balance off the amazement
I must have felt, being only eight—
allowed up late
beyond late in the face

of that wonder, all that light.
The trees sang as if the world had taken in
and changed and was returning
whatever sweetness might have lain

buried at the heart of all that fire,
and though it was the smaller event
by far, it burns
powerful in my memory as the sight

of that thing in the sky.
I'll take it to the grave.
I don't know why
I should remember it at all,

for that trees might sing
ought to have seemed
in the face of so wild
a presence, no equal wonder,

had borne nothing of terror
or disbelief—and surely
there must be things I ought
from duty of love better

to remember, for being
dearer to me, and yet are lost,
gone out, lost forever,
forever have not sung back to me.

—from *Cardinals in the Ice Age*, 1987

Earth Tremor, the Sky at Night

In the smoky light-mix of the sky
above Los Angeles, over the frond-bursts
of the canyon palms, the night
is ready—fog moves in,

and we look up to see
what we think to be stars,
swollen bodies of saffron light
exceedingly too near,

but which turn out as usual to be
no more than some bright diffusion
of the literal, this time
street lights on the far rim of the canyon

seen through fog. Not far away
the sea bed dives beneath
the raw edge of the continent,
the house shivers, our reflections

double in the window, and we look out,
steady ourselves to see,
and the weather lifts and thins
so that everything out there reveals itself

in all the common light, such
as the true stars at true distance dwindle to, such
as the companion body dwindles to
once its weathers clear.

—for Alfa-Betty Olsen

—from *Cardinals in the Ice Age*, 1987

The Weather

After ten days of rain, the heart
cannot tell if it is too young

or too old, is unwilling
to decide, does not know,

refuses to say.
After twenty days it learns

that even in daylight, if only slightly,
the window reflects the wallpaper

and that to lean toward the glass
is to see it whiten and go dead.

Damp Rot

Water sheets on the old stone, fans out
over the cellar floors in little deltas of mud,
worse every year so that by now
there is daylight at the footings, upstairs the floors
have begun to tremble and the clothes
go damp in the closets. The whole place seems
about ready to collapse, and I have begun
to consider moving, unaccountably sad
at the thought of leaving this house
which has possessed us for eighteen years,
in which one of us has died and two been born,
for all its elegance of detail
most everything not right in it or long gone bad,
nothing done

which should have been,
one hundred years and more
of water rancid in the cellar, moldings
mitered crookedly, all the small
and growing energies of dirt and rot
wherever we care to look.
But I also consider the pine grove
of my planting, the green truth
of this place: in one day ten years ago
I dug fourteen small pines, wrapped their roots
in wet burlap, dragged them down
from the topmost ridge of Bean Hill,
spaced them carefully, watered them each day
for one whole season. Now

they are twenty feet high, thick roots already
at the cellar wall, vigorous and loud
even in little winds, only the resident hemlock
mournful and reluctant to do much in the way

of increasing itself. Still, it is clear
that if I do not freely leave this place
it will fall on my head—though as Ray Reynolds says,
digging at a powdery floor joist with his knife,
there may be more here than I expect, better
than a two-by-six at least, sliding his blade
two inches until it stops at what he calls
the heartwood, meaning, as I take it,
at the wood which has not yet given way.

—from Weather-Fear, 1982

Bad Weather on Blood Mountain

It is cold on the top of Blood Mountain, almost
the verge of snow, and I am bored
because my friends have gone down before me
and my fire is almost out, have begun to imagine
that I am not on Blood Mountain
but on Everest, the Climber torn from his holds
and swept by the terrible snow plumes
of the Summit. I imagine my mask

carried away, my eyes
frozen instantly into a million perfectly hexagonal
lenses of ice and I stare at a million hands
from which one by one the fingers crack in little bloody
hairlines at the knuckles and break away.
I find it strange

that there are no visions. I feel myself
being slowly buried by the wind, the snow is up
to my thighs, my chest, and soon
I am breathing snow, asking myself
when I will grow angry, hungry, frightened,
want love? After this for all time
whenever I lie down, Mount Everest
will heave beneath me, roaring with ice and stone,
its snows exploding from the raw peak. But now,
    thank God,
the weather improves a bit, the rocky sky
softens and begins to drift to the east
showing gold and yellow where

the clouds crack and break away. The wind turns,
Blood Brook is beginning to clear.
In a few hours I will be able to see again
over a northern forest of beech and maple,
leaves mostly shed, the colors of rock and lichen.
This is a hard climate,

but not relentless. I hesitate
on the steep hard spine of the trail, wanting to go neither up
nor down, and then the rain stops entirely, and directly
before me, thrust up through a sudden towering of white
    clouds
the sun appears, and it is trailing a great wind plume
of gold and yellow fires, and still I cannot decide.

—from Blood Mountain, 1977

At the Top of Blood Mountain

On the first day of December I climbed
to the peak of Blood Mountain
and found it furry with clouds. I smelled on my fingers
the smoke of the fire I'd built
with red maple chunks and cedar splits,
watched the water of Blood Brook begin
to descend, felt the black mold at the trail's edge
warm almost to fire with the slow rot
of leaves. It grew hard to breathe,
resting there at the end of the path,
staring out into the raw and smoky mists
between me and the next peak. I suspected

I might feel better if I drank from Blood Brook,
or slept for a time in the warm
trail side soil. Instead, I found myself
a hemlock to lean against, breathless. I heard
the faint cries of the climbers behind me
who would never arrive.
Then, as the sun hardened
and began to organize the sky, red yet
as a maple fire and burning
with the same slow difficulty,

I began to think how from that hemlock where I stood
at the always and unbalancing center of
the rooted hemlock, I was in some regard of time
forced to the descent of my difficult breath.
Staring straight up the trunk into the perfect
spiral climb of the branches to their
terrible conclusion high over the mountain
I thought crazily of descent,
of a whelk's shell, God's-eye, spin of maple seed
of the hemlock's green needles that outlast
the winter. I stood unbalancing

into the right of time at the eyed
and rooted center of Blood Mountain
in the precise middle of all that green
and stony, winged, embracing, clawed
and calling out of which surrounded me, and fell
into the one fixed center of theretofore not
present always and beloved
you.

—from *Blood Mountain*, 1977

Van Gogh Prophesies the Weathers of His Death

One morning I will awaken
from the dream of which I did not see the end
to the visible logic of a sky
clouded and threshing with stars,
then find myself unable to close my eyes,
and stare helpless into the slow
opening heart of the sun. And then

as the terrible light widens
and comes finally to bloom
in the fiery shades of the cypresses,
it will seem to me that the young trees
are moving, as if
to a light wind. Or it may be

that one night, alone
in the spaces of the house my body makes,
the last partition of the heart attained,
and all the clocks gone out,
I call out and am not heard,
wait for a little, call again,
in no despair, thinking I see the moon
move in the radiant clouds which are
in reality the cypresses—and for a time at least,
at least for the measure of this time,

I do not die, I am not
entirely unhappy, thinking
into the enormous roar and uprush of light
which has possessed the work,
how nothing has troubled

the beauty of the world, not
the bare eye of the night
nor the eye's first gathering,
not the first rising of the breath,
nor the last,
not even the dream without color

on which at last my eyes will close,
for which I have this long time
prepared myself, whispering

into my dry teeth, moved
to the strangeness—how

after all the turbulent fluidities of fire
I have seen the sky to be,
it should have been the one thing
most like light, the way
the slim branches of the young trees,
themselves nothing like light,
with the wind among them turned and brightened.

—from *Vivaldi in Early Fall*, 1981

Earthquake

                    I am up late, and happy
        to be the only one awake
watching a garish
shard of moon, two planets skirting
        the Adirondacks, the lake
                just visible through bare maples
        shimmering skyward, everything
becoming quieter

                        and quieter, upstairs the sleepers
        staying asleep, when abruptly
the windows bulge, I hear
        a loose sustained shudder and gusting

which I in my startlement unreasonably
                assume to be some huge exhalation
                      of the lake, though it grows and
glasses dance and ring
in the cupboards, pictures swing
askew, the floors commence

to roar, then as suddenly
                  everything simply settles, and I say aloud,
        familiarly, through a sifting of dust

Earthquake! as if all along

        I have been expecting it I say its name
            without astonishment, as if
all along I have been expecting
                so enormous a stirring . . . meantime
           the sleepers upstairs of whom
        I cannot say what so incuriously they dream
remain untroubled to awake.

Foote Brook

At the foot of the slope down which
we faltered, the night roared, the brook
being in full spate. Unbalancing
we leaned into pliancies of birch,

caught ourselves against
the pitchy hemlocks. Then
before we quite expected it
we'd breathed spray—

we were almost there. Because the moon
excited to light the edge of a cloud
the brook at the falls leaped for an instant
with radiance—though elsewhere

light did not abound, nor would we
at that moment have said
night had by ordinary canon come
upon us. The brook was no more

than a minor brightness, yet its voice
was a powerful spasm of the night,
and the large world everywhere
so bountiful an irregularity of surfaces

we could scarcely keep our feet.

—from *Cardinals in the Ice Age*, 1987

Landslide

        By first light the pines struck down into the meadow.
Only an hour before the clouds had been heavy, shadows
            buried the rafters, and light scurried
      window to window. But then
           the snow began to flicker, clouds to deform,
    and from the incandescent line of the peak
proceeded a ragged scrolling of light, finally
        the sun itself clearing the highest ridge,
            bearing with it a wind so violent
      that nothing in the stunned world knew more
           than that something must have changed. At 5 a.m.,
the house cold, cold light billowing and the hibiscus
      abloom in the north window, dark clouds low,
           gold-bellied over the snowy yard, the sky
      paling and bold against it two engorged blossoms
    back-lit by snowshine, star-hearted purple-to-vermilion
        where the petals overlapped, I looked up at the mountain
and from just beneath the shoulder of one shimmering ridge

        occurred an abrupt enlargement of shadow
           from out of which the mountain stormed,
      bearing before it colossal froth of mud, boulders, trees,
      bright explosions of brooks and ponds, snow clouds, all
soundless, therefore suggesting nothing of danger
      so that I felt no need to run
          before the landslide until at last
        it cascaded over the head wall into the valley
and crested in a roar of dust and snow
at the road's crown and overran
the house where I had been standing at the porch window
      brave with amazement. Too late
I discovered myself to have failed
      to escape, to have been borne down
          by house and mountain, my cheek
      crushed into a sour linoleum, my breath
          irretrievable, on my eyelids ant,
earwig, spider, the house above me still
      and orderly in ruin that theretofore most ordinary
         of all mornings when merely to have looked
up at the mountain from the swollen buds
and blooms of the hibiscus, of all things red
      most red, had been enough

                    to commence the overbalancing
           into that swirl, billow, upheaving dome
of ice and shadow where I was about to die,
      or was already dead, or must describe
which it was to be.

                                   —for Don Sheehan

Waking from Nightmare

My timid cat, unhinged by something—
shadow of door frame, fringe
of comforter—claws free of
her dream, hisses, flies
scrabbling across the floor to squat
and calm herself by pissing the rug, as is
her miserable custom.
I gasp upright,

stare out into a sky
shattered and made wild
by treetops threshing in the orange light
flung up from the GE parking lot. Once more
I have dreamed badly
of what loomed irretrievable
even as I dreamed it,
remnant of some appalling consignment

of remorse and blame. I sit till daylight
braced wary against the headboard,
while underneath the bed, exhausted,
recomposed, the cat
purrs and licks her fur. And when finally
I can see, there
is the neighborhood just
lightening, just
settling, of the last
shudder of the dream just barely quit.

Black Dog

Just before dawn today
the yard is empty, no sign
anything prowled there
as all night and every night,

beneath the window
loll-tongued and grinning, in
and out of the long shadows,
any time could have leaped

through the moony glass,
been on me in a flash,
and what might I have done,
who would have feared him more

than ever he loved me?

Devil's Hole

The story goes,
said Saša to me, *that in the great past*
right there in that cave
you forever inattentive fail to see,
himself the Devil came to wish to die,
forgot about God, forgot
about you and me, wished to die
from ordinary pain from loving
a woman did not love him, which problem

he have not anticipate, being Devil
and used to his way. Oh,
but the terrible whore of his predicament
assails him yet! cried Saša, *after this*

he is no worse than us, was nought
for him you know but keep on
loving, him being as we know
one stiff in his convictions!
Then, as we swept

into the big curve, Saša hollering
There she is, Devil's
Hole! I missed it yet again, the dusty
roadside foliage everywhere alike,
black stumps of guard rails
flashing past, dust
and rusty cables, shadow

on shadow, the cliff
a powerful green surge, and somewhere
or other Devil's Hole. *This time,*
cried Saša wrenching the car
onto the shoulder, *I stop*

and you will see! and urged me out
into the dusty roadside brush
into the green shadow of the cliff
to see for myself could I catch out the Devil
who had forgotten not only me,
but also to hate pity and to cherish envy
and likewise horror of roundness
and abundance, in the full

mortifications of love skulking
in his elusive roadside hole
yearning for her, forever beyond

the disposals of mercy. So I stood
quite possibly close by, peering and staring,
but hard as I tried saw precisely
nothing, only drab camouflage
of hawthorn and alder. The sun

low over my shoulder, I squinted
into my shadow, alert
to its diminishment into the thickets,
up on the roadside Saša pacing and pointing, the car
idling on the road, the light
by the dusty leaves broken, broken, and rebroken.

—for Saša Rainer

The Fire

At dawn, furious, I dreamed of smoke,
felt like revenge, like screaming, suddenly
was awake to the room
layered with smoke, couldn't
breathe, knew that the rage
had been terror,
shouted at everyone *go,
get out!* my wife
hauling at doors, the kids, the dog

frantic on the stairs. But they ran
out into the calm yards,
and I was left alone, there
in the unnatural heat of the stairwell.
I closed my eyes and unerringly blind
made my way down into the cellar hole,
and found when I opened my eyes again
that it was like facing the one thing

still alive besides myself, to see
the fire heaving up from behind
the sill. And at the precise moment
that I confronted it, it exploded upwards
into the space between the walls. I knew then

that this fire had been waiting for me
for a long time, through all the years
of my sleeping and waking. I choked
on the deepening smoke, and there

in the swampy cellar faced
the fire at last, appalled
to see it so joyously caper and dance and fly
into the tender darknesses between
my walls. And afraid to go closer, I thought
it is all going to burn now! and *why not?*
After all, it has always been that way,
the dull nucleus of fire locked
into the basement beams of whatever house

I've lived in, working
its slow way out, though that
was the first time we'd surely met.

I stood with a too-short garden house
ankle-deep in the cellar mud,
and tried to wet the timbers down. The fire died,
flared up, subsided, reached

for the floor joists and the hemlock lath.
The light bulb dimmed, the useless water
splattered on hot stone and steamed,
the fire blossomed, and I shouted and I shout
into the darkness and the crazy flames
go out go out go out go out!

—from *Blood Mountain*, 1977

The Morning News

A village boy is down
on the white road. Beneath him,
at first glance his shadow,
is another boy, already dead.
The first has reached out
to intercept the bullet,
in the instant of this photograph

just fired, so direct a gesture
as to be invisible, fixed nonetheless
by the camera as the boy's hand is fixed
light ruddy in the webs, palm clutching
a pulp of shadow, pink rinds of fingertips, fingers
a fan of bones. Day springs up
in trees and flowers of scarlet light,

and I think of the unmemorable small violences
from which mostly I have healed: forehead
bloodied on a tree limb, palm
thorn-gouged, cheek ripped
by a twig, once my right foot gashed
by a sliver of glass hid deep
in the narcissus bed, left breast

crookedly incised, why, when
and according to what process
of small correction now escapes me, but stitched up,
then deeply knit, then knit
ragged, edges overgrown
to proudflesh. For just now
a bearded figure in a jacket
dark with this morning's rain has risen
from among the gravestones one hand
brandishing a wreath of red carnations, to hurl
into a flower-wielding crowd

grenades, then stand intent and curious—
so little general skill have we at resolution, and he
surely one among us, wondering
*how many of the bastards did
I get?* So that this morning
praise blossoms difficultly,
while scarcely beyond the thinning edges
of the particular light creation snarls.

The Recognition

Before the photograph of the hostages
milling in the snowy yard, I lingered
until the guide called out,

and could not for the life of me
think who must have been the one
listless in the middle rank,

propping himself against the pocked wall,
featureless, white-shirted, bald,
among them all he so stood out to me.

—from *Cardinals in the Ice Age*, 1987

The Revolutionary Museum in Ljubljana

Row on row of double photographs, before-
and-after, images so direct
as to invite study before horror,
a dozen or so hostages, some women
in aprons, an old man scratching
at his thigh, all fairly casual, for perhaps
it was the first occasion, and none
chose to know what it was all about
or did not understand
the protocol, or figured it
for a bluff, or simply

went on thinking about the taste
of bread from dinner still
on the backs of their tongues, the smell
of cooking fires, autumn leaves
drifting everywhere. The crowns
of the big chestnuts billowed
in the background, dogs yawned
under the wagons, children
clambered on the walls—but then
in the interval some huge

and unrecorded violence would have taken place
and next they would be lying
as in the throes of some terrible dream,
legs and arms wracked
askew, heads flung

back wrenched sideways every
one of them the mouth
sprung wide. The children
would have vanished, and the dogs
would be looking at the camera, friendly
and attentive. I had to take on faith
the trees were ripening
their fruits. It is not too much to say

I came to know everything
we know against ourselves.
But I had not expected
in horror such dispassion, seeing

how nothing followed from what I saw
because I was alive.

—from *Cardinals in the Ice Age*, 1987

Barking Dog

From down the road and near the landlord's house
his terrible dog, whose fierce and guardian voice
kept us all close upon our boundaries,
warmed up with a few preliminary snarls,

then barked savage, curious and untiring
the whole night through—two yelps, a pause,
and then unvarying two more. I could not sleep.
Therefore though I disliked at night

to walk through my over-dark and speechless house
and must pass a room where lurked
some uncommon terror once
come to someone lived here in my house

in that room, and died; and then to walk
alone along the cold light-feeding road,
nevertheless I ventured out
into the dog-voiced night, angry to be afraid,

when just at the corner of our properties
the world fell silent, and a great black dog
charged across the yard. He was silent,
he seemed not tentative, he carried

his head low. Of all the dread forms
most I dreaded that! Slowly I backed away,
afraid to turn, our eyes on one another's, till
I thought I might be safe, and flung about and ran.

Thank God he did not follow, only
all night ranged the bench marks of our yards
and barked and barked. This happened long ago
when I was wary of malice, large and small,

convinced, though I could see nothing, that I was seen,
and had not journeyed far in understanding
whichever way I turned was always something
at my back. How was it they who lived

along the landlord's road and in his house
had borne it that long while, that voice
which overwhelmed the world, strict
of measure and extensive

of dominion, and they lived nearer
than I lived? Thus
in the large world peace
has not yet visited! For his voice

which troubled me was strong and large,
and carried far, and nothing
drowned it out. So was set
his measure in my head.

—from *Cardinals in the Ice Age*, 1987

Saying the Names

My name—*John. Norbert*,
my father's. My grandfather's, *William*,
David, my brother. *Margaret, Patricia,
Kathy, Julie, Euphrasia,*
the women of my family. Uncles,
James and *Bill* and *Vincent*.
Laura, Leon, grandparents. My mother
Eleanor. Gail, my wife, my

children, *Jessica, David, John,
Laura* and *Matthew*. The dead son,
Philip—all the names
said for the saying, the plain
acknowledgment. Outside

all the waiting for names—
the sun rising, the lakes,
the still fields filling with snow,
whole days filling
with the dull syllables of pulse,
the watch in the breast pocket
louder, more regular than the heart.

Always, more than anything, I wish
to say the names, even
with my dead before me
I say the names
into the bright, breathable air, all the names
of our uncommon time
beating in my tongue, myself

beyond their possibility, awakening
in the middle of the night, breath
regathering, the uncommon
breath—and the last
loud syllable of what I take to be

the one great general name I never hear
just dying in the room, just
whistling backward
to the utterance.

—from *Vivaldi in Early Fall*, 1981

Great Grandmother

Old and awake in her bed
at the Nicolet Home for the Aged
she wanted to die. I did not know her,

having come with my father to visit her
this one time. But I'd wished
she were not blind

so she might have seen
the blue Fox River
from her window. The room

smelled of sulfides from the paper mills,
and red zinnias. *"Norb, I'm old, I
want to die!"* She called me

by my father's name.
I cannot recall
telling her my name. I know

I did not want to die,
having as yet
no sense of power in such a thing.

—from *Vivaldi in Early Fall*, 1981

Wakeful at Midnight

Do you pray to be safe,
rendered without interest
to whatever in your house, hiddenly at play
and otherwise incurious, might pause

in its doings, consider, sharpen its notice, horribly
attend you? How readily on stairwells
do you turn your back? On cellar doors,
on the unlockable closets? Do you live

in terror of the coldnesses of attics?
Midnights, certain the unearthly light
moves room by room closer to where
you have failed to sleep,
how can you not believe

that the darkness flowering about you
will soon pose limits to itself,
that you will be sought out?

—at the Frost Place, August 1989

Ghosts

The looming thing
that moved against me all night long
still lives in the hallway when,
shoes in hand, I limp to the door

and peer out. Then through the wings
of sluggish shadow that it is
spread bright fragrances—
sweet breads, bacon, eggs frying

in the sunny kitchen and I
cannot go down, am frightened to go down,
seeing I have dreamed all night

of birds, of the dogs
of my growing up, my mother
at twenty, my father

among soldiers, thinking
I would hear their voices
for the last time; and hearing them.

For Philip Stephen Engels   August 23–October 24, 1965

Swarming by your head
red plastic butterflies
danced patterns on their strings
because that night you cried

and would not sleep; and I
in my dark room rejoiced
to think that bright beasts moved
to the measure of your voice.

The sun came red as wings
to fix the swimming dust
in all our rooms; my son
your caught voice moves in us.

The house drowns in its lawns.
We watch the morning sun
thrust deep into the sky
a quick and bloody tongue

and in that roar of light
you sleep. Above your head
the blazing wings grow dull
and larval on their threads.

You were no voice at best.
I measure what I tell:
the housed and swallowed bone
grows hollow as a bell,

the breath swims in the throat,
the sun rings in the sky.
What color we remember
burns inward from the eye.

—from *The Homer Mitchell Place*, 1968

Distances

It is the final grief, how color echoes in the eye
from distance, in its cold perspectives.
I see a child in a red hat and jacket walking down
the line of the severe fences
through a snowy field and spare bristle of weeds
till his brave color dances
random on the retina, and blots.

Ghosts walk in color where the brain most dazzles white
and strains at distances the eyes refuse,
fearing that fierce geometry that angles sight
to the utter point the blood eludes.
O the children die beyond our seeing, always,
having outwalked color, having moved
beyond the shadows of the farthest trees.
Our eyes break on the fearful residues.

—from *The Homer Mitchell Place*, 1968

After Thirteen Years

"... looked back from the high hill
on the place I used to live ..." ——Ma Rainey

Snow is falling, the roof flowering
with new ice, and in the house
the closets succeed themselves
one on diminishing other
to the tiny locked heart
at center. The names rise

in little gathering densities.
It is snowing, the sun rises
into the dead center of the sky,
and everything is white:
under the snow the rocks, dirt, tree roots—
this late at night the body,
weak on the side
which does not lean upon the world,

yearns for exactitude in things,
feels the silence in the creature, waits
to want to sleep.
And at this moment, the snow falling
and building, I begin to hear
the small wings of your heart
beating away. In a little while

the sun will tear free
from the white cloud of the earth,
the pines on the hillside will stand out
against the white hill,
morning will surge in, and I will see

ice, pines, the derangement of Vermont
into mountains, the snow fields
stretching to beyond the farthest
imaginable north. The doors

will fly open, and the house
fill with cold, ice
roar from the roof. On such a day
I held you, only an hour born,
your eyes bruised from the first
blunt stun of the light, small blood

exulting into smaller voice—
and felt most powerfully the sundering
of bloods, took you to be,
as yet unnamed, proof
of the short day and the long
shadow. As for the rest, you died.

If you had lived you might have come to see
how, wishing to die, the body swells and grows;
have come to be startled
by the accidents of celebration,
might even perhaps have come into the voice
which cannot be startled into celebration,
have come to believe
that at whatever distance we care to imagine
there is only the pale light without shadows
the snow gives off at night,

only the recollection of voices
from the deep center of the house,
without much conviction
in the way of pain. I wake up

frightened, hearing myself
frantic to say one last thing
into the air of Vermont,
whispering to whatever
at that instant might seem to require
recognition, but lacking
a usable breath to discharge
what I, even at that moment,
will consider a duty. Light bursts

from the tips of icicles, cardinals feed
in scatters of red shadow on the snow:
you come to me from wherever you have been,
but if I turn
to the touch on my shoulder
there is no one—I don't understand
how it is my mind exults
into this elaborate, clamorous voice,
as if I were in company with you

among the gathering celebrative dead, our blood
upon the root. I do not understand
how I can have continued
to name what it is I see,
having named you—except that I know

I have seen you
walking across the field along the fence
toward the pines
into the white field, wide-legged
on snowshoes, the orange bulge
of your pack—though it is not from here

you seem to have left, you are walking away
at precisely that middle distance
at which I begin not to see
you will surely return
hours later, smelling of wood smoke, your shoes

soaked, a glove lost, neglecting
to close the door behind you, the ugly
pale cold of the fields
flooding in.
And I begin not to see

what might have been your eye
encountering the young light
of the fields, your foot
on fresh snow—slow course of seed
beneath the snow, vigorous
green sprouting
from the severed parts: today

comes a soft down-spinning of new snow
and I try to speak to you,
there at the dead center
of the snowing sky: may another
warmer season yet contain
the voices you did not hear, the shapes
on which your hands
will never rest. For now

there is only the cold, slow turn
about the center—look back
from the white field
on the place you used to live.

—from *Vivaldi in Early Fall*, 1981

Anniversary

Ash and maple turning,
the scarlet clusters of the high bush cranberries
hauling the twigs down, tiny
raisins of fox grapes, and the flower stalks
of the monumental rhubarbs six feet high—not

that where I might wish to live it would be
forever balmy, flooded with sun, the hills purely green
and the rivers giving off blue light—only
that in such a place nothing would seem ever to have been
utterly given up, as here in Vermont
in early October, a more than ordinarily dank sun
brightening the soft scrim of the fog,

much seems to have been given up, enough
to make me wish to weep that I could have believed
the last breath taken could be given back, could have been
so stupidly ignorant of the possibilities of loss
to which every morning of my life I had,
thinking it or not, dangerously awakened—though
    only once

to touch it, to see with my own hands
the body empty, the blue bruise
of the baby's body, though why
this should come back and continue to come back
I do not know, having thought, even proclaimed
to those myself among them weary of it
it is finished! that everything

has after all been said, that it is
after all the common practice, one stillness
among the terrible many—even measured it

against the Polish fields blooming with bodies,
the sweet gray breath of Auschwitz, the children
of my time squalling and ready, folded in their fathers'
useless arms, taking the rock, the club, the bullet
in their mouths, and found it
wanting—in the balance thought

I had disentangled the cold grief at such clarities of injustice
from the general rage I am accustomed to feel

at all turns of the flesh, or—in the greater period
of the lesser vengeance—of the world: as in the instance
of the brilliant shadow of October sweeping over us here
and blazing crazily among the trees on the hillside
behind the house, a light

arisen from the flesh of the ice-bearing earth and apart
from what I by birth and all reason
have undertaken to understand as light. Or
in the waking to such a light
as this morning after a killing frost
to a golden haze of alder and willow, the yellow
fog swollen up from the river, a bead of ice
blazing at the edges of the panes, I
have awakened thinking in the face of this light

how could I not have known? even
in the dark as I lay in my bed
about to sleep, and the child's cry
came and when it came
was nothing, nothing, only
the ordinary voice in its
unexceptionable lament
from some darkness of the old
and powerfully retentive house.

—from *Weather-Fear*, 1983

The Silence, for John

The one child having in manner of speaking fled,
his brother ran out to the porch to call him back:
Philip! he cried out, *Philip!* I caught him up
thinking if ever the dead were to be recalled

it would be in similar voice flung confident
into the raving light. Since then
each fall when the woods have darkened with color
the horror has been absurdly to wonder

if I in my sternest father's voice
had commanded into the bloodied gullet of the day
Come back! Come back! he might have heard.
But up on the hill

the pines had strained to a power of wind.
Come back! I might have cried, but I did not,
and silence stormed. Meanwhile
he is speechless, dark, of no intent.

—from *Cardinals in the Ice Age*, 1987

Artesian

1

When, as now,
because the pump has shorted out,
the well is dry,
I am unwilling to believe it

and a dozen times a day
reach out, twist on the tap,
expecting bright fullnesses of water
to swell up in the pipe.

and rush over my hands. Instead
I am each time newly startled
by the quick back-hiss of air
through valves, check-valve

and pressure tank, the frightening
soft suck and in-
breath of the long
down-draining pipe.

2

To my conviction it is always there
bellowing hundreds of feet
below the house,
the river, which has not

ever to this day gone dry,
not even in the hottest summer,
the longest drought—
though when I lie awake

and listen for it,
I hear nothing, only
from somewhere deep
in the deepest parts of the cellars

of the houses I have lived in, slow
tricklings of seepage
into the sumps, at times the slow
trickle and thump of ear-blood.

3

Upstream vague issuance,
the inconsiderable source.

I see an open, marshy corner
of low meadow, a cold

upwelling through schists
and serpentines, blue
glacial clays and muds, a rusty
water seeping from thickets

of cattail, marsh marigolds, trickling
through cress and duckweed, falls
of willow, alder hells, then
the first poolings, minnow-

flash, bright riffling
of streambed, sunlit
flight of the caddis, first narrows
of the true channel—

4

Again and again
I find myself standing
at the sink, opening
the tap—rush

of house air down the dry
well pipe, my very
breath drawn down
into the inaudible convulsions

of the river deep
beneath my house,
gathered and howling
through glassy arches

of rock, black flumes
and conduits, hugely
roostertailing, its voice
one I've listened for

my whole and sleepless
life, its light—
were this river to be light—
what every day I would
awaken to, see by.

Long Ago

one fiery halt dawn
my mother lay by our wrecked car,
still in the savage roadside grasses
a scarlet sop of linen
to her forehead,
and in a soft,
embarrassed voice said
oh please
    don't look at me!
          said that
to me, her fragile own, in whom
close, close to the rendable surfaces
the like bloods perilously kept.

A Little Night Music for My Mother

The tasseled lamp shades
        tremble. Far below the house
                water is on the move. Every surface

            is peaceful, except for the mirrors.
                To west and south blank sides
of a neighbor's house,
                long downpitch

of hillside, dimnesses

beneath lilacs, increasingly
        an eye which sees

             and what is worse knows

Nothing here
                remembers, nothing
        believes the dead can truly
            have loved us.

        They are nearly forgotten,
            yet everywhere the darknesses

of early winter stir aside
            meantime
        the telephones, cords trailing
                over sad, flowery carpets
call faintly
        as if in distant rooms.

The Warning

Every morning there is a conflagration
of twenty peaks
and the sun flies up from behind them
growing hotter and smaller,
straining to disappear
into its vehement heart.
Nearly as old

as my dead mother, I cannot keep myself
from warning her she is about to die. All day
I consider strategies, suspecting the dead
to be set in their ways, difficult
to warn, and warned,

probably scornful. Though I recall
no detail of her face, only
a smudge of eye or of nostril, perhaps
the shadow of a hand,
I am desperate
to be understood. But at night

we are caught between existences.
Though she does not fail
to listen, she seems not to hear,
and speaks to me at all times

in her most ordinary voice
about nothing at all.
Whereas the knowledge I propose
lacerates my tongue,
her calm voice answers *nothing*
nothing nothing

I Dream of Roy Hanna

with whom one morning at a crossroad
outside Peoria, hitching east
from Reno to South Bend, I fought,
then traveled on with, parted from,

and never saw again, until last night
when I dreamed of waiting with him
in that cold dawn, exhausted, stranded
hopeless for a ride eleven hours, the sky

reddening, line poles and wires
taking shape, his face
resuming shape. I dream
of the night-long shrilling of wires,

the two of us, no more
than silent clumpings of shadow,
furious with waiting,
lurching together,

bumping, one or other thrown
off-balance, in an instant
enraged, swinging, glaring,
dawn light spilling everywhere—

of the slow revelations of place,
of us in our slow emergences,
who have not met since then, except
this once where the road is empty.

—for Syd Lea

Joyce Vogler in 1948

That beautiful, pale girl with yellow hair
than whom I shall not other love, nor half so much,
stood with me waiting for the Portage bus,
hands in her pockets, collar up against the wind,

and grinned, and laughed. But I
was worried, it was late, the bus
was late, or I may
have missed it altogether, and

my mother would be waiting up,
and I would not see this girl again forever—
and that has been
the terrible slow truth of it, not wish, not love

recalling me to that night when the wind,
sweet with catalpa blossom, swelling
and softening, drifted her yellow hair
across my face, broke sternly on us. Now

in the monstrous wake of passage I give up
to no less love than did not understand before
the flesh intent on its timely bearing.
The night hums crazily with wind and trees,

birds fly as if it were full day.
I see her laugh, I look away,
I crane to see the whole black empty length
of Portage Avenue—and there at the end

is the late, the final bus
ablaze with yellow light
just turning out from the billowing night
at the far end of the street—for always

time worried me, though always
I was home in time.

—from *Vivaldi in Early Fall*, 1981

The Palais Royale Ballroom in 1948

Just at the end of the first set I step out
in my white tux, my white shoes
onto the sequined dais at center
into a golden spotlight, another focused overhead

onto the spinning mirrored ball,
spills and whirls of gold light everywhere
like stars, like comets hurtling across
the blue cloth ceiling of the Palais Royale Ballroom

in South Bend. And I wait,
Kenton and the boys riffing quietly behind me,
Milt Bernhart disconsolate among the brasses,
June Christy waiting, even June, for this

is mine to do alone and everyone
knows it and everyone
is waiting. And then
I see out there beyond the light

the dancers begin to take notice, to turn,
gather themselves into a circle around me,
arms linked, swaying, others, little
eager knots of them hurrying to get back,

the word having spread even
unto the streets. They gather around me and wait,
knowing what is to come, the air grown dense
with the fragrances of gardenias, camellias, carnations,

the light that is like stars and comets
careening over the ceiling of the Palais Royale Ballroom.
They wait, and suddenly I raise to my lips
the red gold Olds trombone

and hit high G so clean, so sweet, so un-
endurably sustained, that the girls
I am remembering myself to have loved
beyond desire go faint

with desire. The song is "Summertime,"
and I am alone with it, play it out, drive through
to the last sweet resolution of the last phrase.
And then, my solo finished, the great band

riding it out behind me, the song diminishing
into the sky beyond the starry sky
which was the ceiling of the Palais Royale Ballroom in 1948,
my lips still numb from the embouchure, I think of it

as if in fact it might have been that way,
as if those dancers to whom too late and far too late
I have thought to offer this as a memory
might truly have gathered themselves around

and have remembered such a thing: the song
in its starry, high, unlikely register,
the surging of their bodies to that song,
that fragrance of light again.

—from *Weather-Fear*, 1983

Lonnie Peterson

Right here in Guthrie's house, directly
in the middle of trying to light
a coal fire, distracted, it's true,

my guard down, Maeve
for the fourth time since breakfast
at the first phrase of *Für Elise*

in the music room next door,
Owen careering up and down the lawn
dragged by a roaring runaway mower, Bernard

hurried and sharp among
his man-high, ironic foxgloves,
his composts from the bottoms up

transfiguring themselves,
here in Ireland, fifty years after the fact,
Lonnie Peterson presents himself,

pushy as ever, out of some imperative
of coal smoke, green smell
of a cut lawn, gas fumes, flowers,

the insistent tune, fitting time
badly as once he fit his little desk
far back in the classroom, directly

behind mine, where, farting
into his lunch box, prolonging belches
beyond the heroic, beyond

even my huge capacities
for admiration, like clockwork
every morning puking

onto his desk top, pissing
his knickers, he refused to cry.
I poke at the clinkery grate

where the sullen coal no more
than smolders, but once or twice
flares up, as abruptly dies.

The Ghosts at Red Banks

. . . *small hissing rain, white stone*
at the pond's edge, clump
of yellow flag—I've stood here
in front of this house under its big cedar
fifty-eight years ago this very spot
in another understanding. Looking in
at one window I see the spring's
first hatch of spiders scuttling
on the sill, leaf dusts and fly husks, at another
a gray overbrimming light pooled fanwise
on the floor. High in the tree

a widow-maker snaps, brief eddying
of wind and the pond water
clouds and curls, the day thickening
with passage—for I have come to believe
they are returning or even
that they are somehow still here
though more and more with nothing
on their hands but time, and having
forgotten altogether
the gorgeous syntax—they fail
at being remembered—*what*

has happened? Why
were we never warned? Where are we
now? How was it undertaken, how
rightly undertaken, all this
which is left undone? But I
cannot answer, being practically
wordless, seeming to have forgotten
the name for everything, while I suspect
they remember nothing else.
Directly enough

a blossoming of yellow flag.
From a third window, house smells
cascade over the sill—*closets,*
cellar mold, cedar, kerosene—
and across the reflective water, overlaid
on a dull film of sky,
falls the general shape I've made
wherever I've stopped light.

A Watercolor

The paper was too wet—the colors ran.
Greens went olive, blues turned flat
in ways I'd not intended. Blacks and browns
bloomed in little soft rosettes

which bled into the lesser densities of hue,
for lofty in the hierarchies of my error
stood far too great a readiness to let
water do the work, nor had I learned

to love transparency, nor yet
to hold the paper's whiteness
in correct regard—therefore
these failed renderings, dull trees

around the cloudy ponds. I turned away
the better to see out
across the field to where the woods should be.
The woods were night-ridden though a voice

rose at the field's farther edge
something like a rush of leaves.
It was too dark to see, but when I turned
the air shone for a second where my hand

had rested, then transformed itself
into a membrane of green fire
that traced my moving arm . . .
so for a time I paced

gesturing about the room, to see
the light complexly flare and fail—
though soon enough I tired
and came again to the window, wanting air.

—from *Cardinals in the Ice Age*, 1987

The Fragonard, the Piéta, the Starry Sky

1

I am happiest here on the street,
walking with this woman, my hand on her arm,
the sun bright with forsythia,
the great subterranean waves of the granite
cresting in the park—

but in the galleries less happy,
less happy in the private light
where she abandons me to stand
on the far side of the room
to look at the child Virgin
in the early practice of her art,
threading a needle,
the rosy candle suffuse
in her fingers, her face white,
shadowless, intent.

2

I am amazed at the brilliance
of the Northern palette,
the alizarins, madders, lakes
bright in the folds of the saints' robes,
ceruleans clear as shallows
over a white ground.
But not far on

among the jewels, white stocks,
blacks and umbers of the merchants,
shadows take place, and before long
I cannot look anywhere
without wanting to bolt
from the bored, black-stockinged whores
on their sallow beds, the rose nipples
of the Polynesian girls, their baskets

of scarlet berries,
the convulsed cypress that strains
to the star, the lion ravenous
in the cold, viridian foliage.
When it is time for me to leave
she walks with me halfway to the doors,
turns back, and I look after her

small and bright in a blue shirt, climbing
the long stairs back
to the company of saints.

3
I go out into the shining street
and stand for a moment at the fountain
the spray beading on the light hairs of my hands.
And I don't know what to make
of all this joyous, watery display,
seeing I am alone again.
So that when I walk home
the city becomes the spinning-out
of the shadow from whose foot I grow
and which persists.

4
I wake up scarcely knowing I have slept
and the sun which all night
was locked in the stone of New York City
breaks loose, becomes fire,
grows so intense a heart that to look into it
is to go blind in a white dazzle. Then,

little by little, the sun wearies of this burning
and permits the city to rise and cover it.
And at nightfall I witness this descent of fire
and the rising of the streets to meet it,

and feel myself again
at the root of the contorted tree,
at the boundary between light storm
and static rock,
and in the night when it finally comes
I see how the sun allows the shadow
and contains it,
and cry out, impatient
for the star that is hope,
the sunset radiance that is
the body's eagerness.

5
Later, at this achromatic business,
I tell myself it must be that her face

answers to the names of the world,
that I do not know
how the body should be written,
in what flush or ruddiness,
or how to make the hand
translucent with fire.

I try remembering in which gallery
two cupids, spirits of departed lovers,
embraced in a shattered sarcophagus,
bereft companions fluttering tearfully about,
while the smiling Genius of Love
lighted the scene with a nuptial torch.
I take it to be

the law of measure that applies,
love's progress, as in the panels of the Fragonard—
on the white fields of the walls
a mélee of doves and flowers,
the voices of the youthful lovers,
so fair, so fresh, so likely to endure,
abounding to their pink destruction.

I break the great quotidian joy of Fragonard
to imagine her alone before
the paintings, fixed

by the severities of the Piéta,
astonished at the blue callosities
of the wounds, the blue bodies
of the Christ which nothing of moth and worm
shall have to heritage—above all

desiring to be
of that sheer power of love and grief
as Mary, Magdalen, the John
who shudder with tears, the black holes
of their mouths raised to the dead Faces,
their eyes, hands, arms opened
to one another, bellowing, lovely,
loud with grief
forever into the intractable
white fields of the skies *Come back!*

—from *Vivaldi in Early Fall*, 1981

Mahler Waiting

I wait at noon in the summer house
at Mäiernigg, the distant voices
of children unbearable,
the scraping together
of oak leaves, a dog
which has been barking
for hours. That is all. I am

exhausted. Dear wife, I have not been
alone! The afternoon
is exhausted—piano salesmen
bawling over the fences, Wagner
struggling with his coat, Bruckner,
fat pork butcher of a man, Burckhardt
who assured me
that one morning his eyes
would stay shut, and then
he would be forever blind, Schoenberg,
riddler, Pfitzner, your particular
fool—and Wolf, who is dead

in that dead silence that follows
on the stroke of the muffled drum;
finally the child
who is dead, and whose name
I will not speak. *Oh, how night descends
to smother even the holiest
of days!* When I consider how

I believed in the blue flower, the indeterminate
desire, how I wished
that every man might know
by what intent I spoke
to him, how I imagined
that in the end I should have waited out
this air, cold with the coppery smell

of zinnias—dear wife, when I am dead
I will call back to you: *now
the danger is past!* Now

I spend a quiet afternoon.
I am almost well again. I eat

with appetite. I mean to be
in perfect health. But the silence
of this afternoon is

an intolerable thing, when I consider
how by any measure (*breath, eye blink,
heartbeat*) I hurtle in
the vast stellar agitations, by my small weight
the very planet
perfected in orbit. And I

imagine what might be its sudden
catastrophic lurch at my least
miscalculation, shift of weight—clashings
of boulders, trees battering one
another, floods, tornadoes, the fires

bellowing outward from the deep heart
of the world. I want to cry out
Mozart! Mozart! as if it were
the end. Soon enough
will come the footsteps
of the servant who brings me tea,
her stertorous breathing. This place

is high on the hillside
over the house. I look down
through oak-leaves
at the roofs. Sometimes it seems to me
I am falling. For all my vigilance
I am never clear how it begins,
I never know
If I have stumbled, been pushed, leaped.
There is not much more to say—
it begins with falling,

the calling out in mid-air, the cool
choice of stance: flight, or the posture
that will drive the thighbones up
into the heart. In this vision
I am waiting for the bright explosion
which never comes. Well, dear wife,

however Death and Genius arrogate my hand,
I am hungry, it is time.

I watch my fingers smoothing
the white cloth, the table
is perfectly laid, everything
in high order: the knives
gleaming in place, the hard
cold bellies of spoons, everything
fixed in utter space.

—from *Vivaldi in Early Fall*, 1981

A Reading

Looking out through doors wedged open
onto a descending lawn, hard green
as in the final hour before a thunderstorm,
then beyond through a half-arch of willows
framing two cedars, past which

at middle distance rose pines
blue from the first opalescences
of evening haze from out of which
reasonably I might have expected deer
at any moment to advance, confident, grazing
and staring about, behind me

a woman fanning herself, at the lectern
his hair rumpling in the wind
from an electric fan set loud
on a chair beside him, the poet
whom over the fan's clatter and rush
I failed to hear; above all

beside me delicately shifting
a girl breathless to listen,
ardent to set down in a small book
word, line, sentence I strained
to see, finding
the room too dark, her hand
too small and light, and that she smelled

sour, of old clothes, and besides
as if everything
were plain between us, definite
and understood, she
with her forearm tenderly
or fiercely, I could not tell
for certain, shielded the page.

Spring Prophecy

Each year near the beginning of spring
you will think you have found something
that once you had lost, and because it was small
and of little worth, recalled only the losing,

but for that you will weep. It will have the shape
of a dead tree, a broken
bottle, a spring wind cushioning
your face, it will be

yellow as the smell of camphor in sheets,
no more than that. And near
the beginning of spring, snow will hang on
in the pockets of timothy, and water

will spread on the yellowing ice. Corn stubble
will root in orange and brown puddles,
it will seem only an hour
before a warm rain. In the river

a trout will rise under a dark
overhang of cedars, and something
will be given to you, you will have
a vision: one day,

driving to work, you will see
the convergence of the road
to be no farther
than the end of a hallway, no farther

than the far wall of a room, a fog
boiling in the cut, brown
as the smell of old timbers. There will be
a death somewhere, the cellar

of an old house will fill up
with smashed bottles, there will be
a snarl of rotting dresses, papers
spilled down a muddy stairwell. This death

will have been behind you, in another town,
but something will remind you. You will think
you have found something again, but in a day's time
you will have forgotten.

—from *Signals From the Safety Coffin*, 1975

Garden

In May a delicate atmosphere
of willows, and much
that contrives to convince the voice
of itself. In June

the broad leaves of the marsh marigolds
shine a little at the edges,
there being always
some small measure of light.

Later on comes a briefness
of warm rains, then a dimness
among the flower stems
and the orange bells

of squash blossoms,
while on the far side of the garden
one pallid tendril of cucumber vine
wavers up from a yellow chop

of mustard bloom
like the last gesture
of something going under,
which is how, against

all understanding, I choose
to understand it.

—from *The Seasons in Vermont*, 1982

In March

In March begin to think
of the difficult accumulation of days,
the difficult orders
of their accumulation.

In March reappear
from under the snow the gorgeous
ambiguous trashes of the world,
none of them ever more

than the simple work itself,
but never less. Therefore in March
be especially attentive. Be aware
how the day moves out from itself,

and the white spin of the sun begins its pitch
down to the next day, next and next
of fiery awakenings, the helpless resurrections.

—from *The Seasons in Vermont*, 1982

Meadow

Once in late summer I walked into
the tawny, deer-tramped meadow, found

in a crushed-out hollow
evidence of disport, scatter

of clothing, joyous
stink of the bruised grasses—so turned

in sad confusion back, tried
to disperse myself, but everywhere

along the meanders of the brook
arose the warm reek

of cedars, and the willows
flickered with green light.

East Middlebury

With small confidence in skill, gear, or tackle,
years upstream of us, inattentive
and restless to renounce
everything we might have failed
to remember—on that day
of more than ordinarily dank sun
thigh-deep in the familiar river in which
we no longer capably believed,
each pointed out to the other
where at the pool's head had occurred
one tiny rise, upon which came another,

more vigorous, and so on, until before long
the river from bank to bank was lively
with splashes to a hatch of little yellow mayflies,
which at this time of the afternoon at this time of year
we ought to have expected, and to which
short and late we cast, raising at once
three minor trout, then waded ashore to rest
in the strangeness it was to have undertaken

from little hope the old rubric, and by the agitations
of an inert surface to have been restartled.

The Garden in Late Summer

Who among us can truly say
he outlives the thick matters
of cold? Meantime
the world flowers: foxglove,
hollyhock, calendula wrenched
sunward, cosmos by its own weight
downsprawled, cumuli
of marigolds, beaded lily stalks,
curl and shrivel of peony leaves,
lightburst of gloriosas,
and from the beds of alyssum, pink
and white, shastas, dahlias,
all grand manner of rose. Thus
summer arrives, bedizened, decorous,
old, male and uncertain, riding
conclusion, unwilling to last.

Mountain Road

Low on the mountain road
this year as every year
since I first came
to set orderly the new place,

too early in August
and plain before me on the mountain road
overnight erupts
from the same tree
vermilion leaves shaken

with light, at the same time
a lesser light falling
on the road as along
a body of still water.
In such a climate
contradiction lacerates the heart:

I must be innocent
of everything, and yet
somehow exasperate the season
for there before me
is discourse plain enough,
and I continue unwary.

Orchard

By late afternoon the light
had given way and the air
cooled. Mists welled
from the warm ditches,

spilled and merged.
We drove through the topmost layers
of a cloud.
From the door sills up our house

greeted us, though directly enough
we found the steps and walked
sure-footed in, the rooms
settling a little as we entered—

this after a gilt September day
in celebration of itself
spent picking apples
in the Early Transparent orchard,

the air beneath the young trees
dusts of green light, the apples
a fragrant windfall
so that wherever we looked

there seemed to have occurred
in the grass among the strict rows
an exuberant error
of season, a great yield

of sudden yellow flowers.

—from *Cardinals in the Ice Age*, 1987

Pilgrimage

In October on the night of the first killing frost
I come again to the river through the cornfield
above Chapman's Cove, ahead and out of sight
the croaking of the Cove's resident heron. I come

on this night of the first killing frost
as every year to watch the ground fog pour
in soft falls over the lip of the bank. I come
to the surge of the big current through a mist
of birches. The maples of the Winooski

drop their leaves, and the thread of the current
goes crimson, the pools and eddies
churning and frothing with color. I come to sit
on the big rock below the rapids, and find
as usual that the October maples of the Winooski
on the river's far side seem

an impossible clarity of color, a dream
of color, I find
how exhaustible
are the names of colors. Later

I step into the water
that is warmer than the air,
and begin to wade, the river deepening,
rising on my upstream hip, the great downbearing of water
beginning to make itself dangerously felt, and then

and just in time, past midstream diminishing
so that I come through safe
to the pale minnowy shallows and reach out
and pull myself up by the gray roots of maples,
seeing at the top of the bank columns

of rooted clouds, in the top layers
an orange moon shining through. And then
I turn back and look
over the whole dangerous power of the river
translated into a current of fog,
and cannot see the far bank
and stand where I am
until it is wholly dark, afraid

to cross back, stand there
until the moon is fully risen
and the trees shine forth again
as if it were fully day in the last
seasonal burst of the last
color, for which
on this night of a killing frost,
my breath visible before me, I cannot
and do not wish to find a name.

—from *Weather-Fear*, 1982

Vivaldi in Early Fall

Oh this is what it is to be Vivaldi
in September in my forty-eighth year,
the pines just beginning to sing
on the mountainsides, the canals
coloring with the first rains
which are as usual precisely
on time. And there is also

this young girl who each year
I bring into my mind,
making it to be that if she knew
by what measure I considered her
she would turn and look at me and smile
thinking, *It is the priest again,
the one with red hair, who is said
to make music, and who—as every year—
has gone a little sweetly crazy,
and I think he may love how I am today
in my blue dress.* And oh, she
is right. In September I am moved
to that melancholy theme. I like to make the cello
sing with the pines, be on the verge
of the thunderously sad. And as always
at this time I would like to make the melody

go on forever, but cannot, being cursed
to disdain my narrow lusts
and sorrows. I have never said
that with me an innocent angel
is alone at work—it may be
I exercise the murderous grace.
But in September the face of God
passes through my walls to show me
how the motion of song sleeps
at the center of the world, as indeed
among the Angels, innocent of time. I hear

at this time every year the voice that loves me
crying out *return! return!* and I
do, I round on the beginning in full belief—
but the girl is gone, having never breathed
as I breathe, in the weary
exactitude of matter. The song

stops at the certain moment
of its growth. It is
the truth of me, and I
can do nothing with it. Still

it is autumn and over the whole world
the air resumes its liveliness, and I,
Vivaldi, possessed of love and confidence
in measure wonderful to me, I seek
to magnify the text: viola, bassoon, cello,
it is as if the trees have broken into song
and the song roots, blossoms, thrusts
deep toward the still center, overspreads the sky
like a million breathing leaves.

—from *Vivaldi in Early Fall*, 1981

After Alcuin

O my cell, my sweet
beloved dwelling place: farewell
forever! the pines
are resonant with wind,

the peach groves are in flower,
and the fields bloom with wild marjoram
for the free gathering.
The river, its banks brilliant with daisies,

surrounds you, and the fishermen,
as always, are tending their nets.
The cloisters are fragrant
with apple blossoms,

roses and lilies mass
scarlet and white in the gardens,
and one of every bird God ever made
sings morning praises to Him, as once

in this holy place I am about to leave,
my master prayed from his book
aloud, and we novices followed,
joyful, with untroubled hearts.

But clouds double
and redouble. The world shudders
through the slow coalescences of soils
and lights, and prospect

is not sustained. Now
my prayers and songs are full of tears,
for with no warning at all you are lost
to an enemy whose face

I will never know. Never again
will the novices come to sing praises with me
beneath your bright roof. Oh, it is thus
the beauty of the world ends,

and all is swept away: for nothing is forever,
night descends, winter in an instant
destroys the rose, and the young, passionate hunter
who once chased after the stag

across the fields, is an old man
staggering on his crutch. Why
should it be the special nature
of our wretchedness to love most

that which most eludes us, that
which is stolen away?
Why should it be
that in even the most luminous

arrangements of memory,
the bitterest of winds
come to torment the warm
green sea, only an instant before

flowering with sunlight,
an instant before
leaping and flashing with fishes?

The Electric Fence Game

I walked through the stupid milling
of cattle, came to the shining wire
and reached out, not daring

to hesitate, trusting
to catch hold in the dead time
between pulses, grasped

and ungrasped in perfect
dumb coincidence the wire,
and found it neutral

in my hand—a game
in which the free hand
freely dances, so long

as it keeps time. After the first
and risky taking-hold, everything
was safe enough—I looked out

over the calm pastures,
scarcely aware
of how on each side

of the instant of my fist
the blunt stun of the power
licked out. But even

if I had caught hold
and found the wire humming
and alive, that is the moment
I would have understood

how all along
I had desired my heart
to leap and leap in the irregular
dark spasm

and keep on,
would have desired
to give up to the cold pulse of the wire
the lesser power of my hand

to open itself
or not, to splay
out fingers, free itself
of what in love or other

synchronous play
it had chanced freely
to close upon and hold.

—from *Vivaldi in Early Fall*, 1981

Walker Mountain

    All day and night outside his window
the gravel trucks skirt Walker Mountain
        thunderous along the little road
    uproars of loose chains, tailgates,
    downshift, catch
        and strangled bellow
    of big breathing—outside his window

nothing pauses
        but labors on,
    at times the earth
from its clangorous epicenters
    buckling to spring back,
        his bed lurching.

Night after night along the road
        skunks and groundhogs
    scuttle too late for the shoulders
        raccoons double on themselves, he sees
            green eye-fire of the dazzled foxes
            masks and guard hairs bright
        in the truck lights, standing their grounds,
            interested to the end.

        And just where the light not quite gives out

        at times an ungainly bird shape will flush
            from some horrible blot in the median.

    Night after night the dog's red brush,

the vixen's belly fur,
        are felted to the pavement. Mornings he sees
            long smears of gut,
        tongue-blot, eyes
            strung out luminous and green, the clouds
        on Walker Mountain

    masking the sun,
        sliding down to mix
            with the meadow fogs, masking
        the road. Thus
the agencies of ruin that morning

    on chill brilliance of morning
      early and loud outside his window
unstoppably declare themselves—

    nor does he leap
more vigorous with age, nor his life
    resolve itself in beatitudes
      of consonance—moreover
his heart has begun
      the traitorous fat ripening. It seems
   that everything confined
     to the terrestrial duration has begun
to shake into its separate dusts. When at last

    from out of the chill landscapes
      the pines of the east ridge have begun dully,
        dutifully to glow, he leaves the road,

    slogs through the marsh
      forces his way chest-high
   through cattails, tightropes
      the slippery logs bridging
        the little springs, unties
the painter, pushes off and rows
   clear out to the lake's center
      drifts there awhile, the sky lightening,
   withdrawing shadow and reflection,
the woods commencing
    to scream with crows;
      leans over the gunwale,
  face bent so near the surface
     each breath softly forms itself
       onto the water,
    then stares
    into the clarities of shadow his head makes
   stopping light, finding there the downward sparkings
of stars, abrupt deepenings,
  mantlings of oozes, bedrock, then
      reboundings or
  upwellings of the green fire
he has never failed to believe
     burns close on the clean center,
  his face close

        almost to kissing the warm
surfaces, breath halt,
           excited, roughening,
                    more than the fragile last
                                      downward fountaining

In a Side Aisle of Kennedy Bros. Antiques Mall

When I stumbled on the oval print
I was shaken, for it was mine,
having hung at the head of our stairwell
twenty years, before
I sold it. Beyond counting
the times I paused before the very girl
on her beribboned swing, that boy
spying on her from behind
the flowering bush. Nearby

stood the big green demijohn
with its seigneurial seal,
brought unbroken all the cold way
from Wisconsin to Vermont,
likewise cleared out, sold for nothing,

and for a moment I thought
I must have come on the whole of the old consignment,
long auctioned off, and retrieval
might be in the question after all.
But search as I might, I found nothing else, everything
was gone, lost for good, got rid of

in some stupid crisis of muddle and cumulation.
That day, years later, suffering room enough
and to spare, surrounded
by middens of china, clocks, chromos, everywhere
clutters of old glass ringing with light, I stood

in a dusty aisle of Kennedy Brothers' Mall
in the midst of those sad dispositions,
amazed to discover myself

so staggered with loss; at so
desiring everything, all of it,
back again, appalled.

Emergency

The morning wind that blew from the south
through Cedar Grove across the golf course,
carried the stink of winter—the day
nevertheless warm, sweetly proportioned,
a fat, upwelling sun, a ripening light—

though now it is all about to be taken back
that never was freely given
because his heart, swollen to movement
it seems not in disposition to sustain
has called him, and he has awakened

terrified, and awakened the night man at his desk
who has sent for help, which has come
and extracted him to the dark passageways
dazzlements and blindings of corridors,
and rolled him off gaping stare-eyed up
to the intent regard of the head-man's clotted nostrils,
perceived through the pale V

of his own perplexed, embarrassed feet,
the leapings aside of the lobby-dwellers
from the crook of the foot-man's arm, the wakeful
makers-way, nimble
getters-out-of-there—likewise

respectful flingers-wide of doors
beyond the last of which he finds himself
removed to a cold night, moonless
and unstarred, a parking lot excited
to pulses of red light—behind him

the dazzling lobby, at his desk
and registers the night man, those
terrible courtesies, that sorrowful
vast breathing of doors

—South Bend, Feb. 20, 1992

Landlord

We rented. Our house
was the village madman's, very cheap.
He never came around

until one day
in a seethe of July dust,
all tags and tears, the town dogs

in a fury at his heels, we found him
grinning at the door,
as we discovered

we had always feared. *Welcome!*
he cried. It appeared
that from the very first

we had been not far
from his thoughts, never
wholly absent from his heart.

—from *The Homer Mitchell Place*, 1968

Epitaph

I recall the whole of my life, brief
and hurriedly attained, daily live
through everything again, by turns

unloving and aggrieved, yet not
beyond sorrow, repentance,
shame. I think of all

who have outlived me—most
I was not loathe to leave,
a few I was. One or two

were crazy, them perhaps
I loved, though
stayed away from.

And with none was easy.

Naturist Beach

Arms wide to the terrible sun,
        dewlapped, lavender
  and hairy,
        passionately luminous

            against the gray sea, belly
  broad powerful brocades
    of fuchsias and purples, breasts venous
  dun-haired, tipped with dun,

            before which spectacle I,
    far lesser flowering, bleached
            and flaccid, pray though
I know it will not be
    what saves me, may I be
        reborn like that, to such
    ferocity of color
  as that, naked,

    ugly, fearless
        before light, un-
abashed.

            —Hvar, 1985